Quality Management Training Paradigms

By

Larry James Anderson, Ph. D.

ISBN: 1-4033-2859-5 (e-book)
ISBN: 1-4033-2860-9 (Paperback)
ISBN: 1-4033-2861-7 (Hardcover)

This book is printed on acid free paper.

1stBooks – rev. 10/30/02

ACKNOWLEDGEMENTS

I've studied over the past 20 years the work of hundreds of authors who have provided great works in the area of Paradigms of Quality Management. Many of these authors are listed in the bibliography, however, they are only a few of the many authors who have inspired my ideas over a lifetime of study.

An even greater debt is owed to the U.S. Air Force and the men and women who served with me. As a member of this outstanding organization, I was fortunate enough to be a part of a great training program. Many of the ideas in this paper are founded in the knowledge that was accumulated during this formal period of study, and later, supplemented by research.

Additional information was acquired and subsequently added to this volume through the input of the thousands of students I have worked with over the years. As for being a trainer, I've learned that trainers can learn as much, if not more, in training sessions than the trainees. Many fine leaders added substantially to this paper in hope of adding this information to the world. I am tempted to name some of them, but would undoubtedly forget someone and that would be unfair. In my training activities, I am in constant contact with dedicated professionals in many organizations. Their thoughts and practices also are a part of the ideas and concepts presented herein.

Members of the American Society of Training and Development (ASTD) and the American Society of Quality also had a part in this effort. My mentor, Dorothy Webb and my sister Lesa McClain Betts, added invaluable assistance to my project. Finally, and most important in my adult life, my wife Linder, who assisted and supported me in all the time necessary to complete this project.

Thanks – Larry.

TABLE OF CONTENTS

CHAPTER 1

UNDERSTANDING THE CONCEPT OF QUALITY

The goal of this book is to examine and scrutinize various Total Quality Management (TQM) training programs that are being implemented and applied by today's businesses to guide management toward a more efficient operation and organizational decision-making process. I want to point out that the key to quality training is that it is within the intra structure of every stage of business. This comparison is a look at the effect of quality training delivered by in-house personnel. Several training programs were evaluated in this study. Requests for training plans and programs were mailed to over two hundred quality organizations in the United States. As a result of my inquiry, I received a collection of literature from the American Society of Quality, numerous quality technology books, newspaper articles. Internet papers, and responses from companies that either had or had no training program in place. This book will review my results and provide a quality training picture of a program that can introduce a "holistic" approach to Quality Training in the business environment and to non profit agencies.

This Total Quality training research covers an introduction to and definition of Total Quality Management (TQM) in the workplace, and a brief description of its history. We will look at some basics of a TQM training program and the quality tools that are available in a good Quality Training program. We will also look at an example of an in-house Quality Training program from its introduction into the work environment through its implementation into its working culture. The body of this document will provide examples of data collected from Quality Training programs used by some companies and agencies as a part of their daily operations.

We will also look at a "holistic" approach to quality training. In quality management, the term "holistic" deals with the affects and feelings of people in the workplace. According to future forecast, this factor will be a major player in the future of every training program's foundation. I will conclude this project with coverage of all items and areas where data was provided to use towards the implementation of in-house Quality Training programs. For me, however, my quest will

continue to be an ongoing search for quality improvement processes –
as is the nature of Total Quality Management Training.

TQM is a philosophy dedicated to a managerial concept that
improves the quality of products using a quality management
approach to address employee and customer needs. This concept was
originally developed to improve the quality of industrial products and
services. However, since the 1980s, quality management has been
gaining wide acceptance throughout the managerial ranks of many
diverse industries. It is a structured system, designed to create
organization-wide participation programs within s company training,
planning and implementation stages of a continuous improvement
process to meet and exceed customers need. My compilation has
revealed that companies investing in a sound training program to
implement quality management practices have achieved better
employee relations, higher productivity, greater customer satisfaction,
increased market share, and over all improved profitability goals.
Leadership that received these kind of results, interlace quality
training into each stage of their process.

In order to understand total quality in the workplace, one must at least agree on a consensus as to what is meant by "quality." "When pressed to define a painting, a Supreme Court Justice once commented that even if he could not define a painting, he would still know it when he saw it."[1] Quality is like that! Although few consumers would define quality exactly the same if asked, all know it when they see it. This forms the critical point that "quality" is in the eye of the beholder. The "Total" in Total Quality presents a much broader concept than just what encompasses the profitable aspect to a company's objective. It relates to the quality of its people and the quality of its processes as well. The "Training" in Quality Training is a system function applying phases embedded within the quality improvement process the phases are connected and linked in a interlace formation for its successful implementation.

According to Stephen Uselac, author of *The Human Side of Total Quality Team Management*, "There is little agreement on what constitutes quality. In its broadest sense, quality is an attribute of a product or service that can be improved. Although most people associate quality with a product or service, quality is not only products and services but it also includes processes, environment, and people."[2] To many different people and organizations, 'Quality' has been defined in a number of different ways.

Consider the following definitions:

- Fred Smith, CEO of Federal Express, defines quality as "performance to the   standard expected by the customer."[3]

- GSA defines quality as "meeting the customer's needs the first time and every time."[4]

- Boeing defines quality as "providing our customers with products and services that consistently meet their needs and expectations."[5]

- The U.S. Department of Defense defines quality as "doing the right thing right the   first   time,   always   striving   for improvement, and always satisfying the customer."[6]

Just as there are different definitions of quality, there are different definitions of Total Quality as well.   For example, the U.S. Department of Defense defines the Total Quality approach, or TQM, as follows:

TQM consists of continuous improvement activities involving everyone in the organization – from managers to workers – to act with a totally integrated effort, toward improving performance at every level of the organization. This improved performance is directed toward satisfying such cross-functional goals as quality, cost, schedule, mission needs, and suitability.[7]

Consequently, most would agree that TQM integrates fundamental management techniques, existing improvement efforts, and available technical tools, under a disciplined approach that is centered on a continual training improvement process which ultimately focuses on increased customer and user satisfaction.

As of today, there is no one effective standard training program that fits all organizations, agencies, or corporations. However, an effective training program can be described as a "need-based" program, implemented as a combination of on-the-job training (OJT), classroom preparation, and self-paced instructions. It is important to remember that training is an ongoing evolution, and should never be considered as a once-done quick-fix organizational growth strategy for any company's long-term strategic training needs.

Take, for example, an in-house training program. It has great potential. The organizational benefits provided through such a program are its cost savings, increased commitment, self-educational possibilities, and improved leadership skills. An organization's

6

internal customers (also known as the most important part of the organization, its employees) can consistently customize the Quality Training program to meet the organization's exact needs. Such dedicated internal customers can support the efforts to match the needs of the organization and its people to the requirements of a Quality Training Program.

One of the most fundamental elements of Total Quality Training is the ongoing development of personnel. This means education, training, and learning. It is common to hear the terms education, training, and learning used interchangeably in discussions of employee development. It is also common practice to use the term "training" for the sake of convenience. However, there are distinctions with which modern managers should be familiar. This definition of training is an organized, systematic series of activities designed to enhance an individual's work-related knowledge, skills, and understanding and/or motivation.

Training can be distinguished from education by its characteristics of practicality, specificity, and immediacy. Training should relate specifically to the job performed by those being trained and it should have immediate on-the-job practical application. Education, on the other hand, is a broader term. Training is a subset of education; therefore, the term "education" in this sense tends to be more philosophical and theoretical (and less practical) than training, such as understanding the company's philosophy, goals, and objectives.

The purpose of education and training alike is learning. In an educational setting the learning process will tend to be more theoretical, while in a training setting it will be more practical. Whether the point is to have the learner understand "why" or "how to," the point is still to have the learner understand.[8] Understanding is what allows an employee to become an innovator, initiative taker, and creative problem solver, in addition to being an efficient performer of his or her job.

Although education typically occurs in a classroom setting, and training in a less formal environment, there still exist overlapping concepts; such as education can certainly occur outside of a classroom, and training, certainly, within one. It is through education and training that employees who already know how to work harder also learn how to work smarter.[9]

Business Training in the United States

According to an article American Society for Training and Development, in businesses invest more than $45 billion per year in training. However, there are serious questions about how wisely this money is spent. Is it being used in a way that will bring the best results to its organization, or are businesses spending their training dollars in a less-effective direction? The following sections describe the status of training in the United States by job category, sources of training, instructional methods, and types of training in selected industry classifications.

Training Status by Job Category

Industrial firms with more than 100 employees typically have personnel in the following categories of employment:

- Executive Managers
- Senior Managers
- Middle Managers
- Supervisors
- Professionals
- Sales Representatives
- Customer Service Representatives
- Production Personnel
- Office Personnel

Training provided to personnel in the various categories can be compared in a number of ways. Two of the most informative comparisons are percentage of companies that provide training to employees in each category, and the average number of hours of training received by employees in each category. Figure 1-1 compares the percentage of companies that provide training in each category of employment.[10]

Figure 1-1. PERCENT OF U.S. BUSINESSES THAT PROVIDE TRAINING TO EMPLOYEES

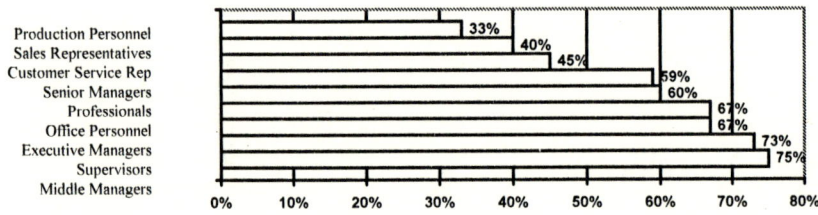

This comparison represents approximate figures for a typical year for companies with 100 or more employees. Figure 1-1 shows that in the United States more companies provide training for managers than for any other category of employee. By comparison, only 33 percent of these companies provide training for production personnel. These figures raise serious questions about how effectively corporate America's training dollars are being spent.

In a Total Quality setting, the philosophy of a TQM's approach to training is based on a bottom-up enterprise in which frontline employees receive top priority in the allocation of training dollars. In practice, this philosophy translates into giving training priority to those employees who are most actively involved in producing products or providing services. The further removed from these processes an employee is, the lower his or her training priority becomes. Followed to its logical conclusion, the Total Quality philosophy assigns the lowest training priority to managers, a reversal of the figures shown in Figure 1-1.

When training data are compared using the average number of hours provided per year per employee, production workers fare only slightly better than office personnel. Figure 1-2 contains these comparisons for companies in the United States for a typical year. Again, these data are for companies with more than 100 employees. When average hours of training are the criterion, only office personnel received less training than production personnel.

Figure 1-2 provides a stark illustration of what happened to many of the U.S. firms that managed themselves out of business in the 1980's. By putting more resources into training sales representatives than into training production personnel, they made a conscious decision to neglect quality. Such a philosophy can be summarized by attitudes such as "Forget quality, just focus on sales." However, Total

Quality philosophy is the opposite, it can be summarized by the

statement "Improve quality and you won't have to sell so hard."[11]

Figure 1-2. AVERAGE HOURS OF TRAINING PER YEAR

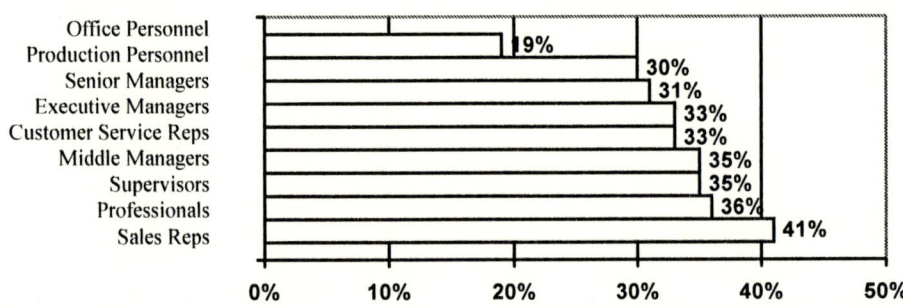

Perhaps we can explain quality efforts as a modification from the

father of TQM, Dr. W. Edward Deming. Looking at Deming's chain

reaction in Figure 1-3, Deming said that if an organization begins

with quality, its cost will decrease because there will be less rework

and errors.[12] The bottom line to this message is with proper training,

the process will improve and the organization will grow.

Figure 1-3. THE DEMING CHAIN REACTION

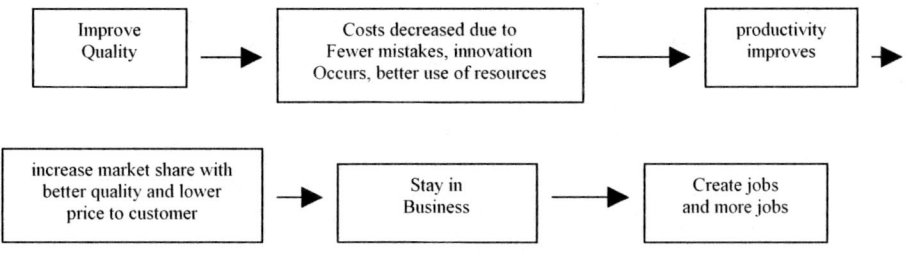

Sources of Training

Many sources of training are available to organizations that want to provide training for employees. Although this section discusses these in terms of broad categories, they are discussed in greater detail later in this chapter. Employee training falls into one of the following categories: internal training, external training, or a combination of the two. Figure 1-4 <u>summarizes the percentages provided using each of these approaches</u>.

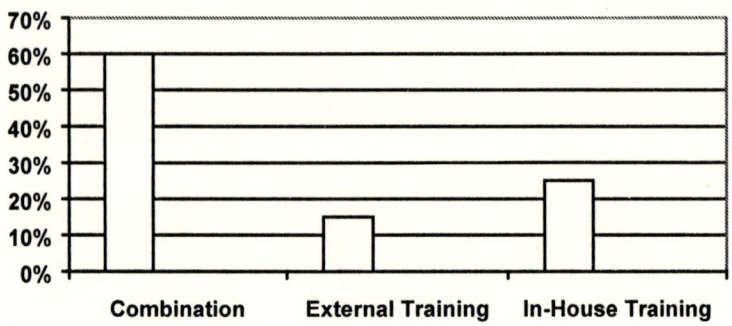

Most training is provided through a combination of in-house training and external sources, though in-house training is the second most widely used option. In-house training is a broad heading which covers on-the-job training, in-house seminars/workshops, on-site media-based instructional videotape, audiotape, satellite downlink, and on-site computer-assisted instruction, etc. External training is a broad category into which we can fit college or university courses; workshops and seminars provided by colleges, universities, and/or private training organizations; correspondence courses; vendor-sponsored training; as well as technical, trade, and professional association-sponsored training.

CHAPTER 2

SOURCES OF TRAINING

INSTRUCTIONAL SYSTEM DEVELOPMENT MODEL

ISD is a model that uses quality process to implement training into an organization. This model is introduced through designing, developing and supporting a training system. It requires considerable time and effort on the part of managers and curriculum developers. Curriculum developers must develop, design, and implement effective cost efficient training, while managers must control, coordinate, and integrate the training into a total quality training system using principles of quality improvement. Total Instructional System Model includes phases, system functions, and the QI processes.

This model has been designed to represent simplicity and flexibility so that instructional developers with varying levels of expertise can understand the model and use it to develop effective, cost – efficient instructional systems. The model also depicts the flexibility that instructional developers have to enter or reenter the various stages of the process as necessary. The entry or reentry into a particular stage of the process is determined by the nature and scope

of the development, update, or revision effort.

The ISD process is a functional design of a total instructional system. Instructional System

Development shows the basic top – level system functions of the instructional system: Which are Management, Support, Administration, Delivery, and Evaluation.

System functions of the ISD model are:

1. Management - the function of directing or controlling instructional system development and operations.
2. Support – the function of maintaining all parts of the system.
3. Administration – the function of day – to day processing and record keeping
4. Delivery – the function of brining instruction to students.
5. Evaluation – the function of gathering feedback data through formative, summative, and operational evaluation to assess system and student performance.

ISD products are integrated into the total instructional system, and

aspects of the system functions are active throughout all phases of the

ISD process.

We will take a look at the phases most often used in the systems

approach, which are analysis, design, development, and

implementation, with evaluation activities integrated into each phase

of the process. The phases are the elements in the system functions.

Evaluation is the central feedback network for the total system.

The instructional development process calls for instructional developers to follow the phase elements.

A. Analyze and determine what instruction is needed
B. Design instruction to meet needs.
C. Develop instructional materials to support system requirements
D. Implement the instruction system
E. Evaluation is a central function that takes place within every phase.

The phases of the model depends on each of the other phases working together.

ANALYSIS PHASE

Based on the analysis a task list is developed from job performance requirements to insure students will have the knowledge and skill for their job. This helps ensure that the customer's needs are being met. The developer then analyzes the job tasks and compares them with skills, knowledge, and abilities of the incoming students.

The difference between what they already know and can do and what the job requires them to know and be able to do determines what instruction is necessary.

DESIGN PHASE

In the design phase, the instructional developer develops a detailed plan of instruction which includes selecting the instructional methods and media, and determining the instructional strategies.

Existing instructional materials are reviewed during this phase to determine their applicability to the specific instruction under development The instructional courseware specialist also develops the instructional objectives and test and design for instruction. The implementation plan for the instructional system is also developed in this phase, and a training information management system is designed, if required. Formative evaluation activities continue in this phase.

DEVELOPMENT PHASE

In the development phase, both student and instructor lesson materials are developed. If the media selected in the design phase included items such as vide tapes, sound slides, interactive courseware (ICW), and training devices, these are developed here. If a training information management system was developed for the instructional system, it is installed in this phase. As a final step in this phase, the implementation plan is updated. During this phase, instructional developers also validate each unit module of instruction and its associated instructional materials. They correct any deficiencies that may be identified.

Validation includes:

1. Internal review of the instruction and materials for accuracy
2. Individual and small – group tryouts
3. Operational tryout of the whole system

Revision of units / modules occurs as they are validated, based on feedback from formative and summative evaluation activities. The final step in this phase is to finalize all training materials.

IMPLEMENTATION PHASE

The instructional system has been designed and developed, and it is now time for the actual system to become operational. In this phase, the instructional system is fielded under operational conditions and the activities of operational evaluation provide feedback from the field on the graduate's performance.

EVALUATION

Evaluation is a continuous process beginning with the analysis phase and continuing throughout the life cycle of the instructional system.

Evaluation consists of:

1. Formative Evaluation, consisting of process and product evaluations conducted during the analysis and design phases, and validation which is conducted during the development phase. Included are individual and small group tryouts.
2. Summative Evaluation, consisting of operational tryouts conducted as the last step of validation in the development phase.
3. Operational Evaluation, consisting of periodic internal and external evaluation of the operational system during the implementation phase.

Each form of evaluation should be used during development, update, and revision of instruction, when if possible, and if the form of evaluation is applicable.

Both system functions and ISD phases embedded within the quality improvement process are connected and linked in a building block formation for their successful implementation. The objective of quality improvement is to foster continuous improvement in the process and products of ISD. It is an independent evaluation to determine whether the products are meeting the users' needs. The objective of quality improvement is to ensure on time- development of high – quality courseware that enables students to reach the desired performance levels in an effective and cost-efficient manner.

This chapter contains seven sections to introduce you to a brief overview of the ISD process.

These Sections are:

A. Total training system functions
B. Analysis
C. Design
D. Development
E. Implementation
F. Evaluation
G. Quality Improvement

Total training system function.

System functions should be in place when implementing a training system. The Roles of system functions are defined below.

MANAGEMENT: The practice of directing or controlling all aspects of the training system.

SUPPORT: Provides for and maintains the training system on a day-to-day as well as a long term basis. Example coordinating the resources you need to keep equipment functioning.

ADINISTRATION: The part of management that does day to day tasks such as documentation, student assignments, and student records.

DELIVERY: The means by which training is provided to students. Instructors, computers, printed materials, audiovisual programs are all examples of ways to deliver training.

EVALUATION: The function of gathering feedback data through formative, summative, and operational evaluations to assess system and student performance.

For the training system to be effective and cost efficient, system functions must be working before the actual design, development, and implementation processes begin.

A major part of ISD is the Advanced Training System. It is designed to support almost every aspect of the training process, from analysis to evaluation. ATS performs several automated functions, which integrates and automates training through development, delivery, evaluation, and administration.

Another function of ATS improves learning effectiveness through the next list of items.

    A. Computer-based training (CBT) and automated classrooms
    B. Self – paced instruction
    C. Remediation
    D. Instructing, testing, and evaluating to requirement

Through coordination, communication, testing, and evaluation you are able to reduce paperwork. This leads to improvement in instructor productivity by automating lesson plans, testing, and counseling. Another function of surge capability is reducing time required for the completion of courseware. You need to use design, development and delivery of the product to complete this function.

TRAINING SYSTEM SUPPORT FUNCTION:

The Training System Support function consist of the following ISD processes:

    A. Training
    B. Analysis,
    C. Design
    D. Development

TRAINING SYSTEM SUPPORT FUNCTIONS:

. Training requirements and task analysis
. Objective development
. Test development and validation
. Lesson plans, sequence, flow chart and storyboard design tools
. Media modeling
. Electronic publication support
. Automation of course control documents with cross – referencing to requirements and resources.

TRAINING DELIVERY:

. Computer-assisted instruction (CAI) interactive videodisc (IVD) classroom instructor controlled, group paced.
. CAI/IVD classroom-student controlled, instructor monitored
. Instructional aids to traditional instruction
. Student remediation and practice.

The ISD processes supported by advanced training system support using the internal training evaluation must consist of:

A. Students
B. Materials
C. Resources
D. Instructors

You must look at student administration and resource management in supporting your processes.

. Student performance as status monitoring
. Interface with class assignment system
. Instructor performance monitoring
. Scheduling of students, instructors, equipment, facilities, etc.
. Review of training data
. On - line coordination, review, and editing of training documents.

ANALYSIS

During analysis you collect information on job performance requirements tasks, and duties for the targeted position. This tells you how to determine the necessary qualifications of the job performers. You then conduct analysis to make sure you provide the right training for the need. A key point is to conduct the analysis before you begin to design and develop a new training system or revise an existing system. Conducting analysis correctly will provide valid training requirements and accurate predictions for the resource requirements. To conduct analysis, you need to assess items such as:

- Equipment
- Subject matter experts
- Weapon system data
- Technical data
- Occupational Survey report data
- Engineering data
- Similar systems or programs
- Performance standards

The analysis phase includes the following elements:

A. Conduct Occupational / Job Analysis
B. Conduct Task Analysis
C. Conduct Learning Analysis
D. Analyze Resource Requirements / constraints
E. Develop Training plan
F. Update ISD Evaluation plan
G. Update Management Strategies

An occupational or job analysis identifies the jobs which defines an occupational entity and then identifies duties and tasks which comprise of each job. It starts by breaking a job into various duties which are the major segments or divisions of the job. The duties are further broken into tasks that make up each duty.

Before you begin the analysis phase of ISD, make sure you have identified a problem that can be solved with training. Training can solve only performance problems caused by a performer's lack of skill, knowledge, and ability to perform a task. If the identified performance problem cannot be solved by training, do not enter the ISD process.

An occupational / job analysis allows instructional developers to break a job down to a list or inventory of tasks, which will be further analyzed in the following statements. As the instructional developer or a member of a design team, you normally are not responsible for occupational / job analysis. However, you may asked to complete a job inventory or serve as a Subject Matter Expert (SME) for your career field during the analysis. As a manager or developer, you will be using the survey and training extract developer to determine what tasks require training. Data for job analysis can be gathered from many sources, such as:

    A. Survey Reports
    B. Job inventories
    C. SME's
    D. Publications such as regulations and manuals
    E. Contract data

As you can see, there is a wide variety of data sources. Other data sources may be available depending on the occupation or job being analyzed.

Let's look at a outline of a job analysis and some of the areas you should understand in the process.

1. Develop an inventory of tasks that make up the job. To develop an inventory, you should

   a. Review documentation from similar jobs
   b. Use existing training standards for your job
   c. Use SME's to provide detail job information
   d. Observe jobs being performed

2. Validate the task inventory by using questionnaires to collect data from the field.

3. Analyze the data from the questionnaires and prioritize the tasks. Tasks are normally prioritized based on:

   a. Percent of the members who perform each task
   b. Learning difficulty of each task
   c. Training emphasis of each task.

4. Recommend the appropriate method of training for each task such as classroom, on-the-job training, distance learning.

Occupational or job analysis is a highly technical process requiring personnel in various specialized areas such as development of job inventories, and/or data analysis.

DESIGN

Training design is like architectural design. First you must figure out what you want the training to look like and how you want it to work before you build it. The analysis that you previously conducted helps determine the basic structure in the design phase.

Conduct design to save money, improve product quality, and get the training done on time. You don't just go out and start developing training, just as you don't start building a classroom facility without planning and designing it first. Proper design will result in:

. Objectives that you will prioritize, cluster, and sequence
. Tests that measure the objectives
. Training methods, media, and strategies to deliver the training
. A training information management system
. A review of existing material

For the ISD design phase, you need all the products you developed during initial planning and in the analysis phase.

DEVELOPMENT

After you have specified the objectives, developed test, planned strategies and created activities, you are ready to implement your design in the developmental phase. Some of the tasks in this phase include writing lesson materials, producing training media, developing interactive courseware, etc. As an instructional developer, this is where all your efforts from earlier phases of ISD start to come together.

Up too this point you have completed the analysis and design activities and you are now ready to enter the development phase. The development area contains the following items that you need to consider in your process.

. Prepare plan of Instruction
. Develop Training Materials
. Install Training Information Management System
. Update ISD Evaluation Plan
. Validate and Revise Training
. Finalize Training Materials

Plan of Instruction serves as the overall plan or blueprint for conducting training in a given course. In some training organizations a course syllabus is used for the same purpose. POIs standardize training and control its quality

In the design phase, you select the training method and media that best suit your training needs.

At this point, you start developing the media selected to implement your training design.

Developing training materials is a time – consuming and exacting task. Regardless of the media selected, it is essential that you develop a quality product since it is the vehicle that carries the information to the students.

Most individuals will not be involved in designing or redesigning a training information management system. However, you may be involved in its installation.

An evaluation plan is a "Metric" or "Standard" for evaluation of the ISD process and products. It is developed initially in the planning stage and updated through the analysis and design phases.

To ensure that the evaluation plan is effective throughout the life cycle of the project, you need to update it again in the development phase.

At this point in the instructional development process, objectives have been developed, tests written, instructional methods and media selected, and instruction is being developed. Yet there is no assurance the instruction will be effective. Therefore, the instruction should undergo validation to prove that the instruction provides graduates with skills, knowledge, and attitudes to meet job performance requirements. If deficiencies are found in the instruction during validation, they are corrected before course implementation.

Validation consists of technical accuracy review, individual tryouts, after you have validated the training you should finalize the training materials. During this step, you should make sure that all necessary changes are made to the training materials and they are ready for implementation.

IMPLEMENTATION

Before you put the course "on line," make sure the system functions are in place, instructors and supervisors are prepared to conduct and administer the training, and all of the required resources such as personnel, equipment, and facilities are available. Once the course becomes operational, you should ensure that the system continually receives the necessary support and maintenance. Also, periodically conduct an operational evaluation to ensure that the course continues to operate effectively and cost-efficiently and to produce graduates that can meet the job performance requirements.

Another ISD model layout is this simple method to develop training that meets the needs of employees. It also follows a five step approach that takes the guess work out of what should be trained. Each is described below.

ANALYZE SYSTEM REQUIREMENTS. The first step in any training process is to accurately determine just what the job is. In other words, what tasks does the trainee perform on the job. A job/task analysis is the key to this step. However, you form your personnel into teams. The teams contains Workplace Qualification Training Plans (WQTP) that list the tasks and subtasks performed in each job. Use these as the first step in the ISD process.

DEFINE EDUCATION / TRAINING REQUIREMENTS.

Using the WQTP, from teams, determine which tasks the trainee can perform competently and which tasks the trainee cannot perform. Those tasks the trainee cannot perform competently are the tasks where training is needed. The WQTP also lists recommended training for each task; so part of this step is done for you. However, when on the job training (OJT) is listed as the training method, you must determine the specific education and training requirements yourself.

DEVELOP OBJECTIVES AND TESTS.

A good training objective is simply a behavioral statement of what the trainee will be able to do after training is complete. Objectives are the foundation of any training. You must know where you are going in order to get there. The objective also gives you a definition of what competent performance looks like. This provides the basis for testing to determine if the training accomplished what you hoped for.

PLAN, DEVELOP, AND VALIDATE INSTRUCTION.

Since you now know what has to be trained, have the training objective written and have decided on a testing procedure, you are ready to plan the training sessions. This is where the lesson plans come in. A lesson plan is nothing more than a tool to ensure you train the trainee properly and provide the tools necessary to perform on the job. Do a good job in this area and actual training will be easy.

CONDUCT AND EVALUATE INSTRUCTION. When all the planning is done, it's time to do the actual training. Present the training and then evaluate yourself and allow the trainee to give you feedback on how the training went.

INSTRUCTIONAL SYSTEMS DEVELOPMENT (ISD)

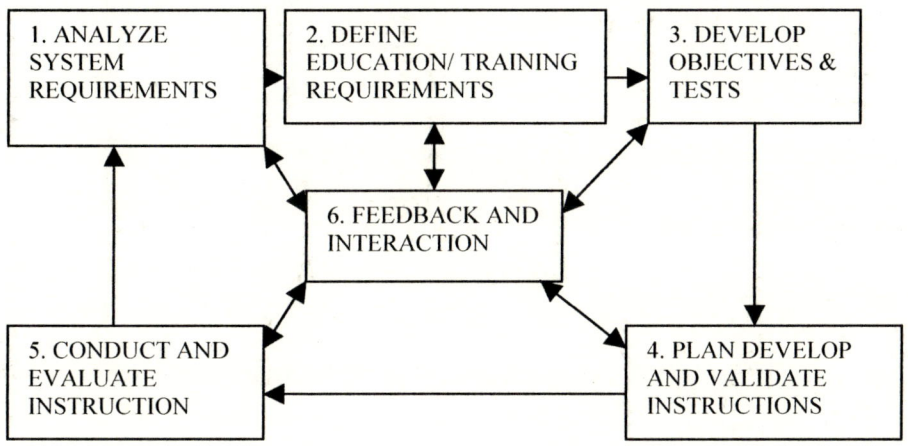

Changing Role of Training

Business training has existed in the United States for more than 100 years. The American Society for Training and Development (ASTD) was established at the end of World War II. It created milestone advancement in business leadership for all industries of management today. The ASTD grew out of "wartime manufacturing businesses that placed a premium on rapidly bringing new industrial workers up to speed on large scale processes and machines that made things."[1]

Since the mid-1950s, interest in corporate training has grown steadily, and is now a part of current and future management strategic programs. Dick Schaaf, a specialist in the area of employee development, worked with the American Society for Training and Development from its beginning. He summarized past, present, and future roles of corporate training in terms of factors such as mission, focus, and vision. For example, he claims that the mission of corporate training has evolved from an old focus on developing skills and discipline to a new focus on improving values and motivation. Future focuses for corporate executives in charge of training, according to Schaaf, will be on enhancing service and quality from inside out.[2]

Training in the United States and Other Countries

The Commission on the Skills of the American Workforce, co-chaired by Ray Marshall and William E. Brock (both of whom served as U.S. Secretary of Labor), issued a report in June 1990 entitled "America's Choice: High Skills or Low Wages." This report concluded that U.S. businesses place an alarmingly low priority on the skills of their employees. A survey of more than 400 companies yielded the following results.[3]

- Less than 10 percent of the companies planned to increase productivity by reorganizing work in ways that call for employees with broader skills.

- Only 15 percent expressed concern over the potential for a shortage of skilled workers.

- Less than 30 percent intended to offer special training programs for women and minorities, although these groups account for 85 percent of all new workers.

- More than 80 percent were more concerned about workers' attitudes than their skills.

- A majority of the respondents said that both employers and unions should have a direct role in the training of workers, but the main responsibility for training and retraining – including funding – belongs to employers. Labor leaders strongly support the concept of a national training tax on corporations, commonly referred to in Canada as the 1 percent levy-grant proposal, to fund training programs. According to Canada's Labor Market and Productivity Center, three-fourths of the business leaders oppose the idea of a training tax.

- Obstacles to improving training include inadequate facilities for workplace training, low interest in training by many employers, and the practice described by the survey report as inter-firm poaching of trained workers.

- International competitiveness is generally regarded as vital to maintaining a high standard of living, but it is valued less by union leaders than by business leaders.

- One-third of business leaders and one-half of labor leaders described workers' reading, writing, and mathematical skills as inadequate. Respondents linked these shortcomings to low productivity, high training costs, poor quality control and difficult recruitment.

- Universities, colleges, and vocational schools do a fair job of preparing people for the working world, according to most of the survey respondents. Elementary and secondary schools were deemed inadequate.

- Although respondents agreed that training was important, they were unhappy with current offerings. Forty percent of business leaders and 86 percent of labor leaders said workplace programs were inadequate.

Why Is Training So Important?

The rationale for training can be found in the need to compete. In order to survive in the modern marketplace, organizations must be able to compete globally. Companies that at one time competed only with their neighbors up the street now find themselves forced to compete against companies from, but not necessarily limited to, Europe, Asia, Central and South America, and the Pacific Rim as well. Many United States companies are like the local high school track star who decides to try out for the Olympic team but then, to his surprise, he discovers that the competition is much more difficult than he ever imagined, and that it will continue to be increasingly so at each successive level, right up to the Olympic Games. Assuming the athlete is able to make it that far, he or she will face the best athletes in the world, not just the ones in his school, his district, his state, or his country. This is the situation in which modern business and industrial firms find themselves today. Like the Olympic team that must have world-class athletes in order to win medals, these companies must have world-class employees in order to win the competition for market share.

Several factors combine to magnify the need for training. The most important of these are: Quality of the existing labor pool

- Global competition

- Rapid and continual change

- Technology transfer problems

Quality of the Existing Labor Pool

Today's labor pool consists of diverse people who are available for, and wish to have, employment. Many jobs are filled from this labor pool. For this reason, the quality of the labor pool is critical when addressing the training needs of a futuristic company. When I refer to "quality" in this sense, it means preparedness and potential of the labor pool. A high-quality labor pool is one in which its members are well schooled in such fundamental intellectual skills as reading, writing, thinking, listening, speaking, and problem solving. Such people are well prepared in terms of the basics and, as a result, have good potential to quickly learn and adapt when put in a working position.

How does the labor pool from which U.S. organizations draw their employees measure up with regard to quality? Consider the following facts released by the National Center for Manufacturing Sciences:[4]

- Youth in the United States spend barely 9 percent of their first 18 years in school.

- Approximately 93 percent of the largest U.S. companies must teach some employees the three R's and other basic skills.

- When compared with their counterparts in Canada, Europe, and Asia, 23-year-old people in the United States place last in math and science.

These deficiencies do not seem to result from the United States spending too little on public education. When comparing the percentage of Gross National Product (GNP) spent on education, the United States ranks among the highest. Of the most industrialized nations, only Canada (4.1 percent) devotes a larger percentage of its GNP to education than the United States (3.5 percent). Japan and Germany spend less than 3 percent. This seems to indicate that though the United States spends more on public education, it gets less for its money than most other industrialized nations. The implications of this situation in terms of the quality of the labor force are serious.

Many U.S. companies must invest training dollars in teaching employees basics before they can begin to deal with higher-level material that will more directly affect productivity and quality. Compare this situation with the Dutch labor force that draws its members from high schools where 90 percent of the students take advanced math courses, or Japan's labor force where 25 percent of elementary school time is devoted to math and science. This puts

U.S. employers in the position of having to spend more dollars in training if they expect to get the same results from their workforce.

Rapid and Continual Change

Change is a fact of life in the modern workplace. It happens fast and continually. Knowledge and skills that are on the cutting edge today may be obsolete tomorrow. In such an environment, it is critical that employees be updated constantly.

Rapid and continual change represents an insurmountable barrier to employees who are not functionally literate to change, as represented by academic performances between grade levels 4.0 and 8.0. The relative literacy of an organization's workforce will determine its ability to keep up. The checklist managers can use to get a feel for whether their organization has a literacy problem is as follows:

1. Do you notice employees having trouble reading and spelling at the level required by The job? (Yes or No)

2. Do you notice job applicants who have trouble completing application paperwork?

(Yes or No)

2. Do you notice employees having trouble using fractions and decimals?

(Yes or No)

3. Do you experience equipment problems because employees cannot read operating manuals? (Yes or No)

4. Do you notice problems in the workplace caused by employees with limited English proficiency? (Yes or No)

5. Do you notice employees who cannot keep up in workplace training programs? (Yes or No)

To understand the number of employees in the United States who may not be able to keep pace, consider the following facts from the National Center for Manufacturing Sciences.

* Almost 30 million adults in the United States are functionally illiterate.

* Approximately 20 percent of the workforce in the United States have a reading comprehension level of eighth grade or

lower, while 70 percent of the reading material in the modern workplace is ninth grade level or higher.

- Approximately 2.5 million people enter the workforce under trained. Organizations that do not provide adequate training may find it difficult, if not impossible, to keep up with the rapid change that is sure to occur.

These facts are part of the rationale for workplace training. There are many companies out there that have no training plan or program for the employees of their organization.

Benefits of Training

In spite of the fact that billions of dollars are spent on training each year, many employers still underestimate the role or benefits of training in the modern workplace. Tom Peters claims, "Our investment in training is a national disgrace."[5] According to Peters, 69 percent of the companies in the United States with 50 or more employees provide training for middle managers and 70 percent train executive-level personnel; however, only 30 percent of these companies invest in training for their unskilled and skilled personnel.

Peters contrasts this with the Japanese and Germans, who outspend U.S. firms markedly in providing training for skilled personnel. Peters believes modern management consultants should understand the benefits of workforce training and be able to articulate these benefits to higher management.

Employers who previously were not committed to the benefits of training but who are now beginning to take an interest in providing it to their employees often debate the applicability or job-relatedness of training. The statement is often made that "We will provide only the training that relates directly to the job." According to Total Quality pioneer W. Edwards Deming; focusing too intently on direct applicability is a mistake. Any kind of learning can benefit employees and employers alike in ways that cannot be predicted. Employers anchoring on job-relatedness are missing the point and thereby losing sight of the overall benefits of job training.

Training Needs Assessment

How do managers know what training is needed in their organization? The answer is that many don't know. When compared with their competitors from other countries, U.S. companies appear to spend a great deal of money on the wrong kinds of training. Based on this information it is top management policy to emphasize leadership training. By placing the emphasis on management, employers are spending the bulk of their training dollars on managing the organization, while losing sight of the need for allocating sufficient funds to include those who actually perform the organization's work. This is akin to training the coaches instead of the players.

This is not to say that managers don't need ongoing training. In a Total Quality setting, every employee needs training on a continual basis. Consequently, the key to maximize the return on training dollars is not to eliminate emphasis on training those who need it most, but to ensure that the training provided is designed to promote the goals of the organization (quality, productivity, competitiveness) to all its levels of employees. To achieve this goal, there are two basic criteria, which need to be addressed by the decision makers of any organization.

The first criterion is simply a matter of reversing the emphasis so that training is bottom-up in nature rather than top-down. Satisfying the second criterion involves assessing training needs. To begin, management must start by asking two broad questions:

- What knowledge, skills and attitudes do our employees need to have in order for our organization to be world class?

- What knowledge, skills, and attitudes do our employees currently have?

The difference between the answers to these questions identifies an organization's training needs. These needs are found by performing training needs analysis. The above questions are examples of some of the questions on a training needs analysis questionnaire. The training needs analysis is the most cost-effective way to maximize the effectiveness of training in an organization. A training needs analysis will also provide quality information about an employee's perception of his/her job role now and in the future. This information is invaluable when developing a training strategy.

Providing Training

When you deal with in-house training programs, you are concerned with the right type of internal training that meets the needs of your organization. Internal approaches to training are intended to provide training on-site in an organization's facilities at a cost-effective base while still achieving company objectives.[6]

There are several approaches that can achieve this goal, such as on-the-job computer-based training, formal training groups, or media-based instructions. One-on-one training involves placing a less-skilled, less-experienced employee under the instruction of a more skilled and experienced one. This approach is often used when a new employee is hired. It is also an effective way to prepare a replacement for a high-value employee who plans to leave or retire and another employee qualified to assume the separating employee's responsibility.

Government and private businesses added Computer-Based Training (CBT) to their plans and this has proven to be an effective internal training company approach. Over the years, it has continually developed so that now CBT is accepted as a widely used training method. It offers the advantages of being self-paced, individualized, and able to provide immediate and continual feedback to learners. Its best application is in developing general knowledge rather than in developing company-specific job skills.

Formal group instruction, in which a number of people who share a common training need are trained together, is a widely used method. This approach might involve lectures, demonstrations, multimedia use, hands-on learning, question/answer sessions, role playing, and mock simulations.

Media-based instruction has become a widely used internal approach. Private training companies and major publishing houses produce an almost endless list of turnkey media-based training programs.

The simplest of these might consist of a set of audiotapes. A more comprehensive package might include videotapes and workbooks. Interactive laser disk training packages that combine computer, video, and laser disk technology are also effective with an internal approach.

An example of a company <u>successfully</u> employing an extensive internal training program is Motorola Inc. Their in-house educational institution is operated through Motorola University, which consists of training institutes for manufacturing, engineering, personnel, middle and senior managers, as well as a center for instructional design. More than 60,000 employees have completed training through Motorola University. It is the company's goal to have a minimum of 2 percent of an employee's time each year spent in training. This goal is another aspect of bringing an organization under the Total Quality Management umbrella.

Evaluating Training

The purpose of training is to improve the knowledge, skills, and abilities of its employees and, in turn, the overall quality and productivity of the organization can become more competitive in a changing business environment.

In order to know whether training has improved performance, managers need to know three things:

- Was the training provided valid?

- Did the employees learn the intended training?

- Has the learning made a difference in employees' job performance?

The following evaluation can be used in every aspect of formal training. Evaluating training for validity is a two-step process. The first step involves comparing the written documentation for the training, such as course outline, lesson plans, curriculum framework, etc., with the training objectives. If the training is valid in design and content, the written documentation will match the training objectives. The second step involves determining whether the actual training provided is consistent with the documentation. Training that strays from the approved plan will not be valid to the organizational goals. Conducting student evaluations regarding the quality of training received immediately after completion can not only provide information on consistency but also on the quality of their training.

Below in Figure 2-1 is an example of an instruction-based checklist

that allows students to evaluate instructions taught.

Figure 2-1. STUDENT EVALUATION OF TRAINING

On a scale of 1 to 5 (5 = highest rating; 1 = lowest rating), rank
your instructor on each item. Leave blank any item, which does not
apply.

ORGANIZATION OF COURSE:
1. Objectives (clear to unclear) 5 4 3 2 1
2. Requirements (challenging to unchallenging) ... 5 4 3 2 1
3. Assignments (useful to not useful) 5 4 3 2 1
4. Materials (excellent to poor) 5 4 3 2 1
5. Testing procedures (effective to ineffective) ... 5 4 3 2 1
6. Grading practice (explained to not explained) ...5 4 3 2 1
7. Student work returned (promptly to delayed) ... 5 4 3 2 1
8. Overall organization (outstanding to poor) 5 4 3 2 1
COMMENTS:

TEACHING SKILLS:
9. Class meetings (productive to nonproductive)... 5 4 3 2 1
10. Lectures (effective to ineffective).............. 5 4 3 2 1
11. Discussions (balanced to unbalanced) 5 4 3 2 1
12. Class proceedings (to-the-point/wandering)...... 5 4 3 2 1
13. Provides feedback (beneficial to not beneficial)...5 4 3 2 1
14. Responds to students (positively/negatively) 5 4 3 2 1
15. Provides assistance (always to never) 5 4 3 2 1
16. Overall rating of instructor's teaching skills
    (outstanding to poor) 5 4 3 2 1
COMMENTS:

SUBSTANTIVE VALUE OF COURSE:
17. The course was (intellectually challenging to
     elementary) 5 4 3 2 1
18. The instructor's command of the subject was
     (broad and accurate/plainly defective) 5 4 3 2 1

19. Overall substantive value of the course
     (outstanding to poor) 5 4 3 2 1
COMMENTS:

Determining what employees have learned is a matter of building
evaluation into the training program and job performance.
Employees can be tested to determine whether they have learned
training objectives. If training proves to be validated and employees
have learned job-related task, then training should make a difference
in job performance, resulting in the improvement of both quality and
productivity in the workforce.

Managers can make determinations about performance using the
same indicators that told them training was needed in the first place.
"Can employees perform tasks they could not perform before the
training? Is waste reduced? Has quality improved? Is set-up time
down? Is in-process time down? Is the on-time rate up? Is the
production rate up? Is throughput time down?" These are the types
of questions managers should ask to determine if training has
improved performance.

Gilda Dangot-Simpkin of Dynamic Development suggests a company can purchase a checklist of questions for evaluating training programs.[7]

Example:

- Does the program have specific behavioral objectives?

- Is there a logical sequence for the program?

- Is the training relevant for the trainee?

- Does the program allow trainees to apply the training?

- Does the training include activities that appeal to a variety of learning styles?

- Is the philosophy of the program consistent with that of the organization?

- Is the trainer credible and relevant to the needs of the workforce?

- Does the program provide follow-up activities to maintain the training on the job?

Why Training Sometimes Fails

Although training is an essential ingredient in Total Quality Management, training is not always automatically successful. In fact, if not properly administered, training will fail. There are many reasons why training fails when it does: poor instruction, inadequate curriculum materials, poor planning, insufficient funding, lack of top management or workforce commitment.

Dr. Juran suggest some subtle and more serious reasons for training failures:[8]

- Lack of participation in planning by management: It is important to involve people at the line level in the planning of training. However, this does not mean management should be excluded. In fact, quite the opposite is true. Management must be involved, or the training may become task- or technique-oriented as opposed to results-oriented. In the long run it is critical that training is results-oriented, or it will fail to achieve organizational goals.

- Too narrow in scope: Training that is to improve quality should proceed from the broad and general to the more specific. Often organizations jump right to the finite aspects of total quality such as statistical process control, just-in-time manufacturing, or teamwork before employees understand the big picture and where these finite aspects fit into it.

Writing for Training by Linda Harold makes the point that training sometimes fails because it focuses specifically on how to more effectively and efficiently perform a task or complete a process, instead of focusing on helping employees become independent thinkers, creative problem solvers, and committed team players to a changing workplace.

CHAPTER 3

QUALITY PROCEDURES

Quality Training Curriculum

In order for managers to play a leadership role in a Total Quality setting, they must be well trained in what Joseph M. Juran calls the Juran Trilogy. The Juran Trilogy Curriculum involves quality planning, quality control, and quality improvement. A curriculum outline for each of these areas is provided in the following sections:

Quality Planning Training

Quality planning, as the first component of the Juran Trilogy, should cover the following topics:[1]

1. Strategic management for quality

2. Quality policies and their deployment

3. Strategic quality goals and their deployment

4. The Juran Trilogy

5. Big Q and Little Q

6. The Triple-Role concept

7. Quality planning road map

8. Internal and external customers

9. How to identify customers

10. Planning macro processes

11. Planning micro processes

12. Product design

13. Planning for process control

14. Transfer to operations

15. Planning tools

Quality Control Training

Quality Control Training, as the second component of the Juran Trilogy, should cover:[2]

1. Strategic management for quality

2. The feedback loop in quality control

3. Controllability (self-control)

4. Planning for control

5. Control subjects

6. Responsibility for control

7. How to evaluate performance

8. Interpretation of statistical and economic data for significance

9. Decision making

10. Corrective action

11. Quality assurance audits

12. Control tools

Quality Improvement Training

According to Juran, Quality Improvement is the third component of the Juran Trilogy and covers the following topics:[3]

1. Strategic management for quality

2. The Juran Trilogy

3. Quality Council and its responsibilities

4. Cost of poor quality/how to estimate it

5. Project-by-project concept

6. Estimate ROI (return on investment)

7. Nomination, screening, and selection of projects

8. Infrastructure for quality improvement

9. Macro process improvement projects

10. Diagnostic journey

11. Remedial journey

12. Progress review

13. Using recognition and reward to motivate

14. Quality improvement tools and techniques

"As one discusses quality improvement with others, one often hears much discussion about the tools"[4] of quality. Effective quality tools are imperative in assisting management with making fact-based decisions. However, management must be wary of people who believe that "tools" is all there is to Total Quality Management(TQM). There is much more to a TQM culture than the quality tools used. Its tools are only one factor of the whole process. Depending on whom you read – Deming, Juran, Joiner's Team Handbook, or Goal QPC's Memory Jogger – you will find a difference in tools used in every business. In addition, you will sometimes even find many of the same tools called by different names. Therefore, do not get wrapped up in a set list of tools. Just use the list as a resource supply and take from it only what makes sense for your organization.

One way to achieve continuous measurable improvement in the workplace can be realized by using a process-focused approach. One of these approaches uses the seven tools of TQM. However, there are many more quality approaches that can be used in a process to address an organization's individual needs.

CHAPTER 4

TOOLS FOR GENERATING IDEAS

Quality Tools for Today's Training

In a quality culture, measurement and analysis are two vital tools of training in a Continuous Process Improvement environment. Everything within this process should be able to be measurable and analyzable. Measurements might include, for example, suppliers' inputs, transformation data that occurs within the organization, or feedback data from contact with customers.[1]

In a quality environment, data collecting is another very important tool in today's training strategy. In fact, one of the seven categories of the Malcolm Baldrige National Quality Award refers to the importance of data collection. It emphasizes the issue that it is the appropriateness of the data collected and not just collecting lots of data for which a company is awarded its points.

Securing a baseline is another quality tool used to establish beginning points, measure progress toward targets, and identify effectiveness of improvement efforts. Analyzing process

61

performance and process capability to meet customer expectations by listening to customers through various feedback mechanisms will lead to the success of a quality training program.

The Shewhart Cycle, also known as the Ishikawa circle, is a process-focused approach to improvement. This approach is repetitive and is often shown graphically as a circle or a wheel. Figure 4-1 is a quick look at the circle.[2]

Figure 4-1. SHEWHART CYCLE

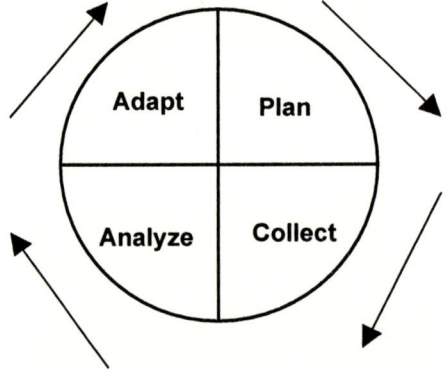

The process-focused approach is the key to achieving continuous measurable improvement in the workplace. The first quarter of the circle is the "plan" phase, which tells management to plan before it takes action. The second quarter is the "do" phase; this is where you put your plan to work. Third is the "study" quarter; here is when the improvement effort is measured, data are analyzed, and results are studied to see if the process was improved or management's target was met. The fourth quarter can help you understand why management did or did not meet its target. Now take "action" based upon what management found in the study quadrant. When management has completed these steps, they have finished one Plan-Do-Study-Act (PDSA) cycle of the process improvement model.

Continuous Improvement Process (CIP) is a systems approach. The seven steps of the continuous improvement process are based upon the Shewhart cycle (Ishikawa circle). While it's true the improvement effort is implemented one process at a time, the overall effect on the system can over-"optimize" an isolated part of a process, which may result in actually reducing the overall organizational efficiency it seeks. Management's efforts may also fail if it is trying to improve a process in a culture that's hampered by fear and mistrust.

Here are the basic steps of CIP:

First, select the appropriate process for identifying improvement opportunities. Second, establish a logical sequence to carry the team through the improvement process. Third, select a process for improvement based on the organization's plans, priorities and data. Tools like flowcharts, run charts, and control charts help a team understand why the process was selected and how the improvement effort supports the organization's goals. Fourth, to evaluate this process, select a challenge, and set a target for improvement. Fifth, help the team focus on the scope of the improvement effort identified in the first step. Sixth, collect, interpret, and analyze data to identify and verify the root cause or causes in a process. Use tools such as check sheets, Pareto charts, histograms, run charts and control charts. Seventh, focus on the root cause instead of symptoms. Employ tools such as cause-and-effect diagrams and scatter diagrams to logically demonstrate the selection and verification of their root cause or causes.

A key phase of the process is to take action to implement planning steps that correct any root causes. Are your proposed actions effective? Are they feasible? Evaluate possible actions to determine if they are effective in eliminating root causes.

Management can use a force-field analysis to develop a plan to implement solutions by using the measurements that identified the improvement opportunity to study the results of their efforts. Pareto charts, run charts, control charts, and histograms can be used to show data before and after the improvement effort.

Tools for Generating Ideas

A tool for generating ideas, called brainstorming, is a popular low-cost mental imaging tool, that is used by many companies to generate fresh ideas. This tool works well for individuals or groups. When management experiments with idea-generating techniques, it is important that they remember that flexibility is a critical aspect of creativity. Brainstorming can generate multiple ideas about a problem or topic and it works well in groups of all sizes.[3]

When brainstorming, a team will write the problem or topic on a blackboard or flipchart where everyone can see it. All ideas are included but not yet edited. Try to withhold judgement until the session is complete. Remember to give the group quiet time to generate ideas: issues regarding owners, customers, and suppliers should also be involved in the process at this time. If you have too many ideas after brainstorming, trim your list with decision-making tools, which will be discussed later.

Another tool that can be used in developing ideas is the "Five Whys" and One H developed technique. The technique is used by management and leadership for problem solving. The five Ws and one H are Who, What, Where, When, Why, and How. This can also be used as a team questioning session to discover the root cause of a problems and how other causes of problems might be related.

Tools for Making Decisions

Decision-making tools can help management keep the process moving once ideas have been generated. Multi-voting, nominal group technique, pair-wise ranking, benchmarking, and force-field analysis are all tools that can help manage the decision-making process.

Here's a guide that can be used to analyze data when groups make decisions. You'll find the type of decision making in the left column. Look to the right for the percentage of group involvement and a profile of the decision style.[4]

Decision Type	Percentage Group	Decision Style
No decision	0 percent involvement	Issue avoided. All members do not discuss the issue.
Decision by powerful minority	20 percent involvement	Decision made by powerful minority or individual. Other opinions are not invited.
Bartering	40 percent involvement	Competing powerful individuals or cliques make "take-off."
Consultative decision	50 percent involvement	Decision made by powerful individuals about the "expert" opinion.
Majority vote	60 percent involvement	Minimal discussion by minority point of view. Minority concedes.
Majority rule	80 percent involvement	Decision by majority vote, but minority viewpoints explored as well.
Consensus	100 percent involvement	Needs and interests of all explored, and unified team solution develops into an action plan.

Multi-Voting

The multi-voting tool helps you separate "vital issues" from "trivial ones" on a large list by finding the highest priority items on that list. This simple but, fast technique works best for large groups and long lists. An added benefit of this technique is that you can prioritize your list without creating a "win-lose" situation for group members.

An example of multi-voting is as follows:

Listed are fourteen items that group members can identify as problems they wish to address. Each team member will have seven votes that they can use to reduce their list to a manageable size.

Here's how they might vote:[5]

VOTES   LIST

|----------------------------1. No agenda
|||--------------------------2. No clear objectives
||--------------------------3. Going off on tangents
|--------------------------4. Extraneous topics
||--------------------------5. Unproductive
|||||------------------------6. Time spent on travel
|||||------------------------7. Money spent on travel
|||||------------------------8. Too much "dog and pony"
||--------------------------9. Problem not mentioned
|||||----------------------10. Unclear charts
||------------------------11. Few meaningful metrics
                        12. Trouble calling home office
                        13. No parking
                        14. No administrative support

As a result of the vote, the group chose to focus on the following problems:
Numbers 6, 7, 8, and 10 were voted as the most important problems.
Number 2 was voted as the next important.
Numbers 3, 5, 9, and 11 as the third.
Numbers 1 and 4 are the least important.
Numbers 12, 13, and 14 are of no importance.

Nominal Group Technique

If your group prefers a structured method to generate and prioritize a list, consider the nominal group technique. This method uses priorities of each group member to discover the overall group priorities.

Benchmarking

This technique promotes breakthrough, and speeds the continuous improvement process. For example, a unit's self-assessment identified opportunities for improvement.

The organization's leaders wanted to focus on those areas needing improvement. What should they do? Try benchmarking! This is the process of finding and adapting the best practices to improve an organization's needs or processes. There are four steps in Benchmarking that are necessary to implement the process. First management should plan and decide what should be benchmarked? What do they hope to gain from the Benchmarking process? Management needs to understand their process and the way they measure that process. The process management selects should support a key result area crucial to their mission and key to customers' satisfaction.

Second, management should identify world-class organizations and compare processes. Management can find possible Benchmarking partners by brainstorming potential sources. It can consider internal experts, professional associations, trade journals, Benchmarking networks, or on-site visits.

The third step is to analyze the data. Study the practices of the benchmarked organization. How do those practices compare to yours? Search for the process enablers making that practice "best in class."

The fourth phase is to adapt the best practices. Consider an organization's culture and infrastructure when management adapts the new practice to their process. However, do not just adopt a new practice to replace an existing one but adjust the enablers to best fit the practice.

Force-Field Analysis

When management needs to visualize issues or concepts that influence their problem or goal, consider Force-Field analysis. This technique identifies and visualizes a relationship of significant influencing forces. Management will be able to identify key factors or forces that promote or hinder their efforts to solve a problem or reach a goal. Management can identify improvement opportunities too. For example: An employee smoked more than a pack of cigarettes every day. His family and colleagues (all non-smoking) wanted him to quit. Despite frequent attempts to stop, the employee continued to smoke. One day the employee sat down with the quality advisor and completed this force-field analysis.[6]

Goal: Quit Smoking

Promoting Forces	Habit
Better health	Need for nicotine
Save money	Need to have fingers occupied
Won't have to leave building	Need to have something in mouth
Family won't breathe smoke	Gain weight when I try to quit

71

After completing the force-field analysis, the quality advisor worked with the employee to prioritize the forces. This helped the employee decide which forces to strengthen and which to weaken.[7]

Tools for Analyzing Problems

Flowcharts, Affinity Diagrams, and Cause-and-Effect Diagrams are excellent analysis tools in providing understanding of the complete process, identifying critical stages within a process, and locating problem areas that exist within that process. A Flowchart is a graphical representation of all major steps of a process. Flowcharts show relationship between different steps within the process. Management can also use thematic content analysis or a Pareto Chart in their analysis efforts.

The first of seven steps to developing a good Flowchart is to define the start and finish point for the process being examined. Second, from the starting point, chart the entire process. Take time to work slowly enough to include every step along the way, right through to the finish. Standard Flowchart symbols can be used to improve the clarity of the Flowchart, but they are not essential. Third, try to identify the easiest and most efficient way to go from "start to finish." This can make it easier to find improvements. Fourth, study the Flowchart. Areas that hinder your process may be discovered. Fifth, check to determine if you've charted the ideal process? Sixth, look at the Flowchart; examine any steps that differ from your ideal process and question why they exist. Seventh, build a new Flowchart that corrects the problems you've identified.

Figure 4-2 shows a standard Flowchart symbols. When management is developing a Flowchart, the goal is to chart the process. Don't waste time debating the symbols. What is important is the usefulness of the Flowchart with or without these symbols.

Figure 4-2. STANDARD FLOWCHART SYMBOLS (AFFINITY DIAGRAM)

Symbol	Meaning	Examples
⬭	Start / Stop	Receive trouble report Machine operable
◇	Decision Point	Approve / disapprove Accept / decline Yes / no Pass / fail

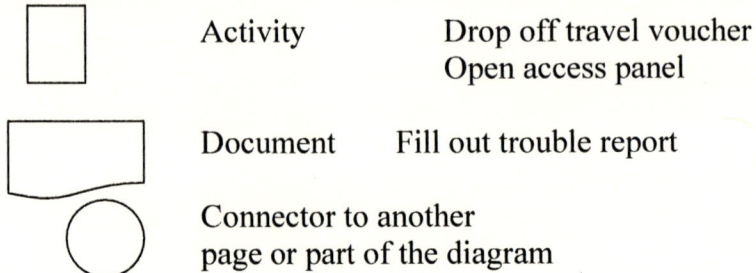

Activity   Drop off travel voucher
                   Open access panel

Document   Fill out trouble report

Connector to another
page or part of the diagram

The Affinity Diagram takes verbal information and organizes that information into a visual pattern. You start with specific ideas and work your way toward broad categories. This is the opposite of a Cause-and-Effect diagram, which starts with broad causes and works toward specifics. Affinity diagrams can also help you identify key areas needing improvement. First identify the problem, then generate solution-oriented ideas. Now management is ready to look at developing the process.

One can use sticky-back notes or cards – anything easy to sort and move. Determine which ideas are similar and which ideas can be connected to other ideas. Questions like these can help you group the ideas. For each group create a card that has a short statement describing the entire group of ideas. Put your group of related cards under the group's affinity card. You can group the affinity cards into broader groups. Keep creating groups until your definition of "group" grows too broad to have a comfortable meaning. Lay out all the ideas and affinity cards on a single piece of paper; you can use a blackboard or table. Put the affinity cards at the top of each group and draw an outline of the group. You'll see a hierarchical structure that can offer valuable insight into the problem.[8] I have used this process on a number of workshops and the results where very successful. Another item is the colored cards that can also be broken up into a frame layout or structure lines. This can also be used to identify groups, sections, and departments by colors. I have used this process in many workshops and teams find this process easy to use and very successful.

Figure 4-3. AFFINITY DIAGRAM

A publications team hoped to reduce typographical errors. Here's the list (generated during a brainstorming session) of factors affecting the error rate:

Computers	No feedback	Proofreading skill	Printers
Noise	Short deadlines	Lighting	Typewriters
Chair height	Comfort	Desk height	Time of day
Spelling	Interruptions	Handwriting	Grammar
Slang	Technical jargon	Draft copy	Punctuation
Distribution	Font	Final copy	Editing skill
Computer skill	Typing skill	No measurement	

The team created an affinity diagram to identify areas for further analysis:

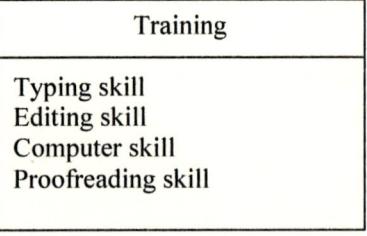

Environment	
Interruptions	**Ergonomics**
	Noise
Unreasonable	Lighting
deadlines	Desk height
	Chair height
Time of day	Comfort

Equipment
Computers
Printers
Typewriters

Training
Typing skill
Editing skill
Computer skill
Proofreading skill

Original document	
Author skill	**Requirements**
Handwriting	Draft copy
Grammar	Final copy
Punctuation	Distribution
Spelling	Font
Technical jargon, slang	

No definition of quality
No measurement
No feedback

Cause-and-Effect Diagram

The Cause-and-Effect Diagram was developed to represent the relationship between some "effect" and all the possible "causes" influencing a situation. The effect or problem is stated on the right side of the chart and the major influences or "causes" are listed to the left.

Figure 4-4. CAUSE-AND-EFFECT DIAGRAM

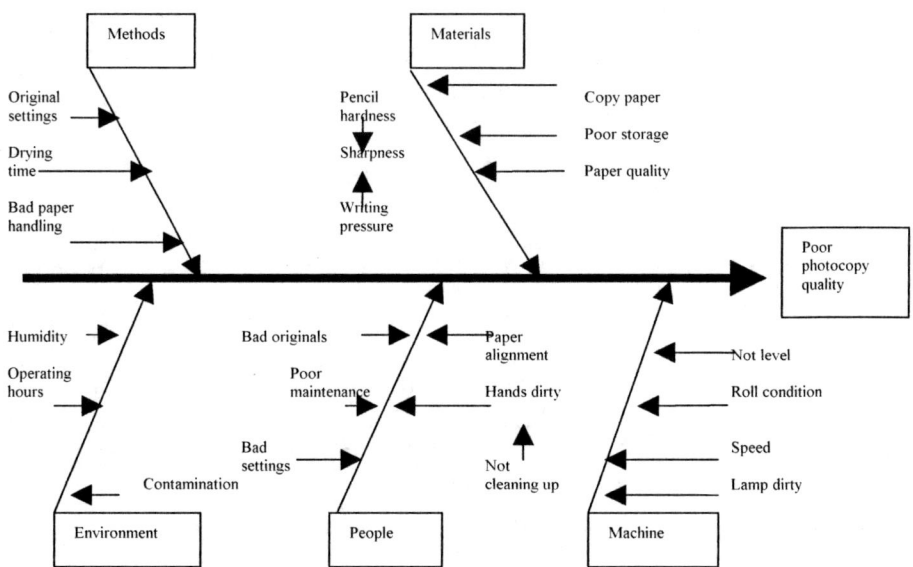

Cause-and-Effect Diagrams are drawn to clearly illustrate the various causes affecting a process by sorting out and relating the causes. For every effect there are likely to be several major categories of causes. The major causes might be summarized under four categories: People, Machines, Methods, and Materials.

A well-detailed Cause-and-Effect Diagram will take on the shape of a fishbone and hence the alternate name, Fishbone Diagram. From this well-defined list of possible causes, the most likely are identified and selected for further analysis. When examining each cause, look for things that have changed or deviated from the norm or patterns. Remember, look to cure the cause and not the symptoms of the problem. Push the causes back as much as is practically possible. Here's what you do to construct a Cause-and-Effect Diagram.

Start by brainstorming about possible causes without previous preparation.

Ask members of the team to spend time between meetings using simple check sheets to track possible causes and to examine the production process steps closely.

Construct the actual Cause-and-Effect Diagram by placing a problem statement in a box on the right. Draw the traditional major cause category steps in the production process, or any cause that is helpful in organizing the most important factors.

Next, place the brainstormed ideas in the appropriate major categories.

For each cause ask, "Why does it exist?" Then list responses as a branch-off of the major causes.

In order to find the most basic causes of the problem, look for causes that appear repeatedly.

Reach a team consensus.

Gather data to determine the relative frequencies of the different causes.

Figure 4-5. CAUSE-AND-EFFECT OUTLINE

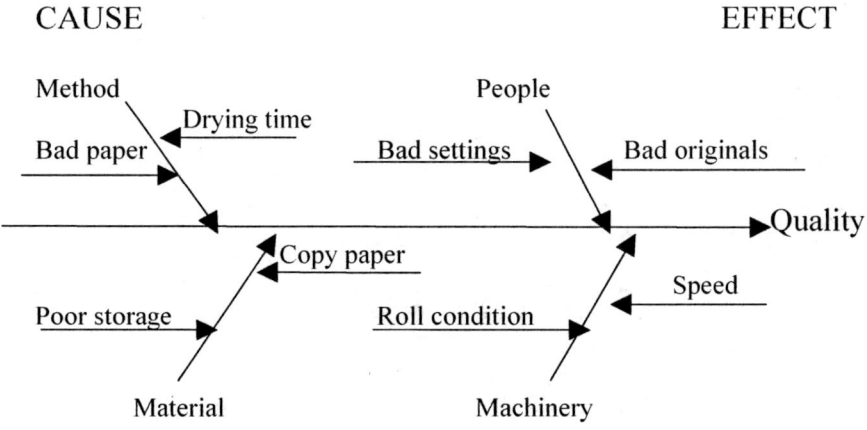

Pareto Chart

A Pareto Chart is ideal for identifying vitally important problems through the use of different measurement scales. These charts are based on the Pareto Principle that 20 percent of the problems 80 percent of the impact. Those 20 percent are the vital few. By separating the problems or issues this way, it helps management focus on the improvement process. Why? A Pareto Chart allows you to arrange data according to priority or importance. This takes the guesswork out of the process, and now management has data identifying the most important problems.

Brainstorming, mental imaging, or asking "why" questions are good techniques for generating ideas. List all the possibilities in a particular process. Management needs to group existing data by consistent units of measure. The units of measure should be put on the left vertical axis and categories of problems on the right horizontal axis. The categories should be placed in order according to their frequency, not their classification. Using a descending order from left to right.

An optional step you can use is the right vertical axis to measure

the percentage of

total occurrences contained within each category.

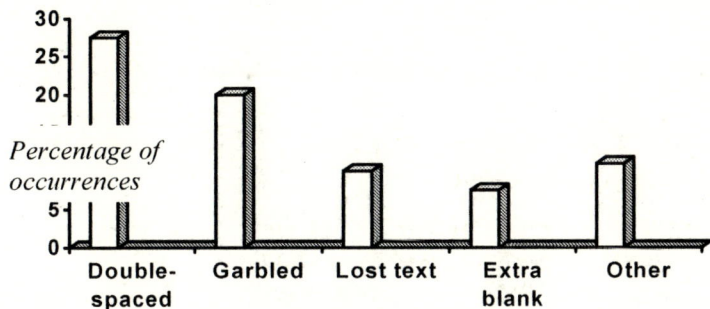

Pareto Chart

CHAPTER 5

TOOLS FOR PROBLEM SOLVING

Tools for Analyzing Data

Management has generated ideas, identified areas ripe for improvement and analyzed problems. Now it's ready to analyze the data.

Check Sheets

When management needs an organized method of collecting data, try using a check sheet. This simple form helps to convert the data into readily useful information. An excellent advantage to using check sheets is they help to translate opinion into fact. With check sheets, management won't have to blindly say, "I think the problem is…" once an organized check sheet has been reviewed.

Pictorial check sheets can give even more information than tabular check sheets. Take a look:

Figure 5-1. RxESULTS OF FINISH DEFECTS ON 100 DOOR

Defect	Tally	Total
Scratch	+++ \\	7
Chipped Paint	+++ ++++\	11
Tar	++++ \\	7
Dent		0
Total Defects		0

B

BB   AA

CCC

A – Scratch
B – Chipped paint
C – Tar
D - Dent

Histogram

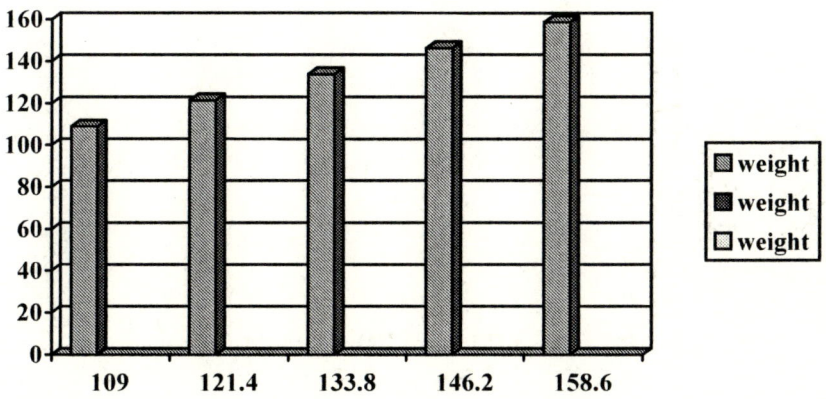

Need to show the central tendency and variability of a data set? Use a bar graph called a histogram, sometimes referred to as frequency distribution. A histogram can help management determine the underlying distribution of a process. It also helps management understand the total variability of a process. When a histogram is used, each "data point" appears in only one interval.

The number of intervals can influence the pattern a data will take. Don't expect a histogram to be a perfect bell curve; instead, expect variations.

To create a histogram, here's what to do:

- Determine the type of data you want to collect
- Collect the data
- Determine the number of intervals required
- Determine the range
- Determine the interval width
- Determine the starting point of each interval
- Plot the data

In addition to the shape of the distribution, management should be looking for whether the spread curve falls within specifications, and if not, how much data falls outside of specifications, or whether the curve is centered in the right place for the organization's needs.

Figure 5-2. HISTOGRAM

Weights of officers

208	180	139	163	159
155	180	165	149	127
159	171	141	190	159
153	181	180	137	161
115	156	173	165	191
159	109	179	145	144
150	206	166	188	165
127	130	172	180	147
145	150	156	171	189
190	200	208	169	139
130	128	155	185	166
165	187	159	178	169
147	150	201	128	170
189	163	150	158	180
139	149	185	129	169
175	189	150	201	175

Scatter Diagram

Management can recognize the relationship between two variables with a scatter diagram. These diagrams are graphs that reveal possible relationships and identify possible causes of problems. (An important note: While this method shows a relationship exists, it won't show the correlation one variable causes on another.) Management will need further analysis using advanced statistical techniques to quantify the strength of a relationship between two variables. Both positive and negative correlation can be useful for Continuous Process Improvement.

The three-step process for analyzing data is to:

1. Collect the data in pairs

2. Construct a graph

3. Plot the data

Figure 5-3. SCATTER DIAGRAM

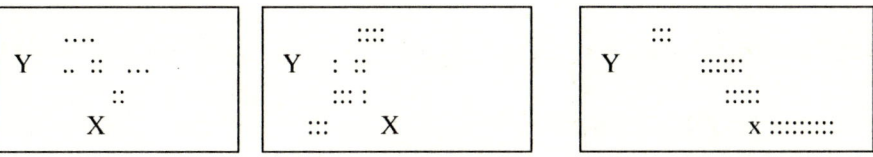

No Correction: Y doesn't appear to be related to X	Positive correlation: Increase in X may be related to increase in Y.	Negative correlation: Increase in X may be related to decrease in Y

Run Chart

To show changes in a process measurement over time, use a run chart. A run chart can help management recognize abnormal behaviors in a process. Label the vertical axis with the key measurement of the process that's to be measured. After all data have been collected, plot each data point on the chart. Average all points, then use this average as the centerline of the chart. Management is to use its best judgement looking for patterns and trends. One signal that may tell management its process has significantly changed is six points steadily increasing in a row. Another possible signal is nine points in a row that are on the same side of the average. Management should re-compute the average for either subsequent blocks of time or after a significant change has occurred.

Figure 5-4. RUN CHART

Number of people on travel

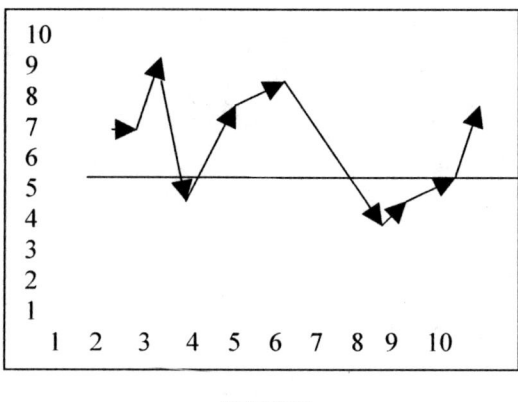

WEEK

Boxplot

A Boxplot, sometimes called a box-and-Whisker Plot, is a graph that offers a detailed picture of trends and variability over time. Boxplots, like Run Charts, help management to see the changes in a process measurement for specific periods of time.

Figure 5-5. BOXPLOT

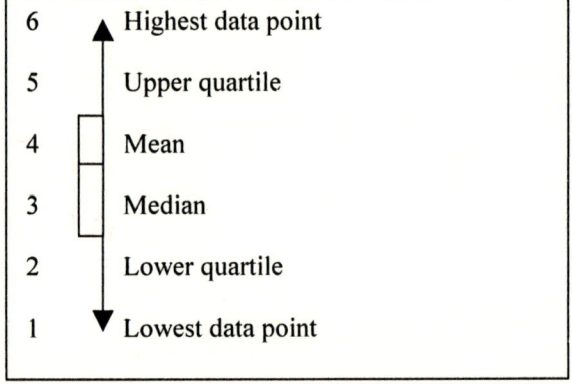

Subset 1 Subset 2 Subset 3 Subset4 Subset 5

Control Chart

Control charts shows management how a process varies over time so that it can recognize, understand, and control variability. A Control Chart can also help management learn how to identify specific causes of variation and changes in performance. Control Charts can be used to help management avoid fixing a process that only vary randomly within control limits. When management needs to address questions such as "Have you clearly identified your process?" or "Do you have data to support an investigation of the process you'd like to control?" with "yes" answers, then it can reach for the control chart.

Although Control Charts are similar to Run Charts, Control Charts can statistically generate upper and lower control limits. A process is in statistical control when the process measurements vary randomly within the control limits, which means the variation is consistent and predictable over time. By the way, don't confuse upper and lower control limits with tolerance limits. Control limits are computed from process information data. Tolerances are specified in standards, drawings and specifications. The relationship between process variation and tolerances is given by process capability ratios; more about that later. Meanwhile, here's a sample Control Chart. Since these charts have many parts to learn, if management is interested in using this technique, then they will need to locate a text that covers Control Charts in detail.

Figure 5-6. CONTROL CHART

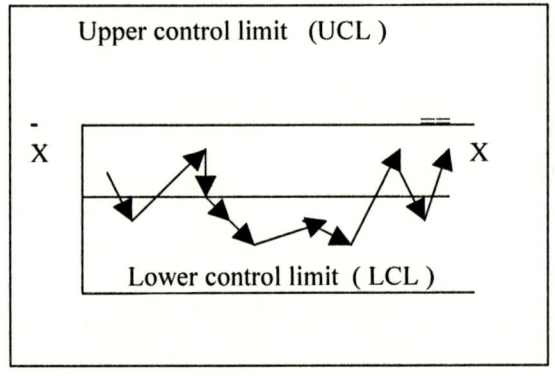

X is the type of control chart. X is a grand average

CHAPTER 6

QUALITY ASSESSMENT TRAINING

Quality Culture

Prior to outlining a training program, let's look at what an organization should do to identify a quality culture and how the elements of an organization are affected by this implementation. A Training Department's first step is to create a baseline by providing a checklist of quality culture characteristics of their employees. Its second step is that of laying the groundwork for a quality culture by activating an environment for change, which will help employees understand what a quality culture is like.

The resistance to culture change is one of the most difficult areas in which to identify and implement real change. The human emotion and its characteristics should be discussed to help complete management's work prior to establishing a quality culture plan. To implement a TQM culture, management should use a timeline to identify where their employees find themselves on a rebuilding culture process. Management should be able to provide a quality

93

culture conversion checklist for the organization. Next, management needs to perform an organizational culture employee assessment survey to assess the existing culture of its organization. The final area is to list the strategies for establishing a quality culture, such as identifying needed changes in the work environment.

The planned changes of a quality culture should follow the steps listed below:[1]

1. Put the planned changes in writing.

2. Develop a plan for making the changes.

3. Understand the emotional transition process.

4. Identify key people to make them advocates.

5. Take a heart-and-mind approach from academics to emotional.

6. Apply courtship strategies and support processes.

This plan should be performed early in the Total Quality implementation process.

Design a Quality Culture

What is a quality culture? A quality culture is an organization with a built-in value system that results in an environment that is conducive to the establishment and continual improvement of quality.[2] It consists of values, traditions, procedures and expectations that promote quality.

To design a quality culture, management must understand the role its organizational culture plays. An organizational culture is an operation of objectives and feelings applied every day to form conclusive underlying values and traditions.

This shows up in how employees behave on the job, and their expectations of the organization. Management should consider what is normal in terms of how employees approach their jobs. For example, the concept that "the customer is always right" may not apply to all with a quality culture. Consequently, what an organization truly values will show up in the behavior of its employees.

Cultural Elements of an Organization

Let us look at the cultural elements of an organization and determine how the implementation of its organizational environment operations deter its culture and affects its environment. Organizations that operate in a stable market in which competition is limited may develop a "don't rock the boat" culture.

Employees know when management is just going through the motions. Changing an organization's culture requires a total commitment and a sustained effort at all levels of the organization. This starts with the value systems of the executives. How managers treat employees and how employees interaction on a personal level contribute to the organizational culture. Expectation at all levels of the organization determines their culture. Communication from employee to employee typically plays a major role in the establishment and perpetuation of an organization's culture. These factors can be positive or negative. For example, when executives treat employees with trust, dignity and respect, and use the golden rule of life, employees will apply the same behavior toward management. Therefore, this action will become part of the organization's culture.

Quality Culture Characteristics

Organizations practicing a quality culture, regardless of the products or services they provide, share a number of common characteristics.[3] Characteristics that can identify an organization's ability to be classified as a quality culture are:

- Behavior matches slogans.

- "Customer input" is actively sought and used to continually improve quality.

- Employees are both involved and empowered.

- Work is done in teams.

- Executives and managers, at every level, are both committed and involved; responsibility for quality is not delegated.

- Sufficient resources are made available where and when they are needed to ensure the continuous improvement of quality.

- Education and training are provided to ensure that employees at all levels have the knowledge and skills needed to continuously improve quality.

- Reward and promotion systems are based on contributions to the continual improvement of quality.

Implement Culture Changes

There are several primary reasons cultural changes must either precede, or at least parallel, the implementation of a Total Quality Program.[4] First, change cannot occur in a hostile environment. Second, total quality takes time. In a conversion to total quality, positive results are rarely achieved in the short run. Third, it can be difficult to overcome failures of the past, because some companies have implemented programs that were not supported by top management and therefore, establishes a history of what employees refer to as a management fad.

The past is not just an important part of an organization's culture, it can be the most difficult part to overcome, especially when many individuals use its failing history to say that new concepts won't work.

Let's take a look at the steps and the processes necessary to implement the cultural change in a total quality environment.[5] First, you must lay the groundwork or foundation for a quality culture. According to Peter Scholtes, an authority in TQM, this should begin by developing an understanding of what he calls the "in accordance with IAW," organizational change. In other words, you need to learn the history behind the existing culture before trying to change it. Second, don't tamper with systems. In order to improve something, you must first understand what is wrong with it, and why and how to go about changing it for the better. Third, be prepared to listen and observe. Finally, there must be involvement of everyone affected by change in making it work.

Since people will resist change, it can be difficult to effect change even when people want to change, without the involvement of employees in planning and implementing the change.

What Does a Quality Culture Look Like?

A quality culture can look like many things that involve the interaction of people, products, and processes. We feel an organization will have the following characteristics, which will describe what an organization is made of and looks like. These characteristics include widely shared philosophies of management that are embedded in celebrated organizational events.

Recognition and rewards for successful employees, effective internal networks for communicating the culture, informal rules of behavior, strong value system, high standards for performance, and a definite organizational charter – these pieces, put together, show what a quality culture looks like.

Paradigm of Change

Cultural change is resisted in any organization. The first step in facilitating change is to adopt a facilitating paradigm. Dr. Juran summarizes the traditional paradigm of change advocates as follows.[6]

Proposed Change	Perception of Advocates	Perception of Resisters
Automate production processes	Improve productivity	Threat to job security
Initiate employee involvement and empower	Focus more mental resources on continuous improvement	Loss of authority
Establish a supplier partnership	Mutually beneficial business alliances	Disruption of established purchasing networks
Establish an employee education and training program	More knowledgeable, more highly skilled workforce	Costs too much
Join a manufacturing network	Enhanced competitiveness, shared cost, and shared resources	Competitors will take advantage of what they learn about us

Steps in Facilitating Change

The steps in facilitating change are:

1. Begin with a new advocacy paradigm

2. Understand the concerns of potential resisters

3. Implement change-promoting strategies.

When confronted with change, human emotion is based on the research that is focused on the stages of transition that people go through when they are confronted with a major, unexpected and unwanted change in their lives. The emotional response is shock. A typical response to the shock is denial. Change is so feared that employees the response is to simply deny that it has happened. The denial phase is temporary, then the realization of reality begins to set in. This can cause depression during the realization phase. When realization bottoms out, acceptance occurs. This is where you can say, "I have a problem, now what can I do about it?" A good attitude allows the rebuilding process to begin. During the understanding phases, people have come to grips with the change. The next step is to explore the quality culture conversion checklist.

Quality Culture Conversion Checklist

This quality culture conversion checklist is designed to provide management with a guide toward turning its organization into a quality culture.[7] Employees assigned to the Best Corporation, for example, are like many employees in other organizations caught up in the mix of change. Some employees support the change. Their behavior is one of wait and see, not belief. Some are ready to learn new approaches, while others feel what they are doing is good enough.

The plan that has been put into writing is called the Customer Product Process Model. The comprehensive plan for making quality changes is being passed down from top management to every level in this organization. Sometimes key employees are not familiar with the emotional transition people go through when confronted with change, but they should be.

Although the role of key employees in the organization have been identified, unfortunately most of the time they are not always on board to make the changes work. Management must create a new team environment which pushes toward positive thinking and action from team members. They must deal with the inevitable emotional response that occurs in the early stages of implementation of a quality culture.[8] We must ensure that the organization is following the plan, step by step, to ensure success.

The final strategy is critical. It means that the material, moral, and emotional support needed by people undergoing change should be provided to all employees. Some units do this well and others need training.

QUALITY CULTURE CONVERSION CHECKLIST

__ Identify the attitude, behaviors, processes, and procedures that are to be changed.

__ Put the planned changes in writing.

__ Develop a comprehensive plan for making the changes.

__ Make sure all change advocates are familiar with the emotional transition.

__ Identify the people in the organization who can either make the conversion work or make sure it doesn't work.

__ Get the key people on the team identified (turn them into advocates).

__ Take a hearts-and-minds approach when introducing the new culture.

__ Apply courtship strategies to bring people along slowly but steadily.

__ Support, Support, Support.

Survey to Assess

I have performed a survey to assess the existing culture of a business I will call Best Corporation. The following is an example of information and instructions from a real survey. The findings will be compared with what is known about quality culture for the purpose of identifying the culture changes needed in our organization for measuring continuous improvement.

This survey was used to determine how some of our groups think and feel about some organizational issues. If money, time, or other resources were not a concern, the most correct data you could get would come from surveying the entire organization. Since limited resources are a reality we all have to deal with, we are often forced to survey the views of only a few members of the organization. Obviously, we want to be able to say with as much confidence as possible that the views of the group we surveyed represented the views of the organization. By using a combination of powerful statistical tools known as inferential statistics and unbiased sampling techniques, I believe the survey and data collected can actually represent the views of the entire organization from which the sample was taken. I use simple random sampling for collection and the sample means process for analysis. I have provided an example of the culture employee assessment worksheet, and a chart of the results on the next page. In the next paragraph you will find a narrative of the assessment results.

The present organization's quality culture has the following characteristics: The strongest belief by the employees is that quality is defined by the customer, and they feel that ethical standards should be important to management as well as staff in every operation. A very high rating was given to executive management for committing to the continuous improvement of quality, product ability, and competitiveness. Education and training are used to improve performance. A normal or middle rating was given to employees who show that they know their role in helping their organization accomplish its mission and participate in its product development cycle. The weak area is that management doesn't treat workers as valuable assets. Employees don't feel they are empowered or that management uses scientific measures for its performance process. The area that was pointed out that needs the most work is continual communication at all levels of the organization. Below is an example of the survey used:

Position (type) _____

Date _____

INSTRUCTIONS

The purpose of this survey is to assess the existing culture of our organization. The findings will be compared with what is known about a quality culture for the purpose of identifying the culture changes needed in this organization to continually improve quality, productivity, and competitiveness. Respond to each of the criteria by circling the number you think best describes our organization as it is today. Zero (0) means that we do not meet this criterion at all. Five (5) means that we completely satisfy the criterion. Do not respond to items that don't apply to you or about which you are unsure.

1. All employees know the mission of the organization	0 1 2 3 4 5
2. All employees know their role in helping the organization accomplish it's mission	0 1 2 3 4 5
3. Executive management is committed to the continual improvement of quality, productivity, and competitiveness	0 1 2 3 4 5
4. Management treats the workforce as a valuable asset	0 1 2 3 4 5
5. Open, continual communication exists at all levels of the organization	0 1 2 3 4 5
6. Mutually supportive internal partnerships exist between management and employees	0 1 2 3 4 5
7. Mutually supportive internal partnerships exist among employees	0 1 2 3 4 5
8. Quality is defined by customers, internal and external	0 1 2 3 4 5
9. Customers participate in the product development cycle	0 1 2 3 4 5

10. Employees are involved in the decision-making process	0 1 2 3 4 5
11. Employees are empowered to contribute their ideas for promoting continual improvement	0 1 2 3 4 5
12. Performance of processes is measured scientifically	0 1 2 3 4 5
13. Scientific data are used in the decision-making process	0 1 2 3 4 5
14. Employees receive the education and training they need to continually improve their performance	0 1 2 3 4 5
15. All employees at all levels are expected to maintain high ethical standards	0 1 2 3 4 5

CHAPTER 7

CULTURE ASSESSMENT SURVEY CHART

The Five-Factor Model

You should have an understanding of other assessment methods used in Total Quality Management Training. The Five-Factor Model of personality does an outstanding job of evaluating personality, team-building, and group growth. Since the 1980's personality psychologists from a range of perspectives have found the Five-Factor Model to be an effective tool for identifying and structuring personality attributes, measuring individual differences in terms of degrees of extraversion, agreeableness, conscientiousness, emotional stability, and openness to experience the process.[1] The model provides a common language for the field of personality psychology, while at the same time it supports widely divergent approaches. How has the model evolved over time, and how has it been challenged? Are these five dimensions adequate to describe the entire range of personality traits? This timely and inclusive volume addresses these and other questions as it explores the Five-Factor Model's theoretical underpinnings, initiating a fruitful dialogue among some of the leading figures in contemporary personality research. Factor models of personality have gone through many transformations, with the number of factors and the designations of those changing, as well as the ideas about how the factors should be interpreted and used in the application. There are two important models with five factors: Costa and McRae's Five-Factor Model, and Goldberg's Big Five. The distinction between these two models lies in how the factors are named, as well as how they are linguistically modeled.

The Five-Factor Model represents the factors as O.C.E.A.N. (Openness, Conscientiousness, Extraversion, Agreeableness, and Neuroticism). The Big Five Model renames "neuroticism" as "emotional stability," and names the "openness" factor "intelligence."[2]

These factors, although similar in nature, are somewhat arbitrarily named. The logic behind them is as follows. The "lexical hypothesis" states that important, salient, and socially relevant individual differences will have a word in any given natural language to describe them (this hypothesis has held up very well for most languages, but failed in a Chinese experiment). Statistical analysis of dictionaries, specifically of the personality descriptive words, can be described as a combination of two of the five factors, somewhere along the spectrum between them. Prototypical words from the categories are chosen to name the factors. Further testing, now of how people report about themselves in terms of these words, has resulted in the theory that these five factors are unrelated (no statistical correlation).

CHAPTER 8

IN-HOUSE TRAINING

In-house training becomes increasingly important as organizations strive to develop workforces to meet competitive challenges. Cost control and organization-specific needs place further emphasis on training efforts. Theses training efforts are a part of the system and tied to the bottom line of businesses.

The development of an in-house training program begins with a discussion of a Quality Training Program and methods to find the part-time trainers necessary to augment the training staff and operations for such a program. The benefits of an in-house program are discussed, along with some of their possible drawbacks. In this way, the benefits can be maximized while the drawbacks are minimized or alleviated altogether.

Quality Training Program

Improving the quality of training and improving training for quality, two distinct and separate entities that must become the highest priorities. Quality Training requires a sound training system, qualified trainers, solid training materials and methods, and emphasis on training from the top down. Training for quality demands an understanding of the broad range of quality subjects, with the training geared to the needs of each particular level of the organization.[1]

Since much of the training required for performance improvements will take place in the work centers, a strong on-the-job training (OJT) program supported by classroom training and self-paced training available in computer based training (CBT) systems, interactive video (IV) systems, and audio-video programs is extremely valuable. This type of program can overcome many of the problems inherent when OJT, classroom-type sessions, or self-paced sessions that are used as stand-alone methods. It is a combination of training programs that provide thorough planning and implementation that pays off in performance improvements.

In many cases OJT probably is the least effective and most poorly organized of all training efforts in most organizations. Suggestions are offered to help overcome the deficiencies that are typically inhibit in OJT programs so that it can become the dynamic change agent that it has the potential to be. This requires a review of the requirements for solid training programs with specific application to OJT programs.[2]

There is no one standard training program recommended for each organization, because each organization is a unique entity. A successful program will be a blend of in-house efforts and outside help. The exact mixture depends on the extent of training assets within the organization and the needs of the people who serve that organization. Flexibility is a key concept in this area. Needs assessment is vital to training payoff and organizational survival.

TQM Training Programs

Total Quality Management training programs that support quality are not once-and-done affairs. It is a long-term part of the process and is critical to success. As each performance improvement begins to pay off, new areas needing improvement emerge and gain prominence, each requiring additional assessment and more training. The pay-off from performance improvements will shortly generate additional profits and/or services that pay for the additional training many times over.[3]

In many organizations, training departments that are not a part of the strategic structure provide much or all of the training needed by their organization. Although this may provide a measure of control and promote expediency, it tends to support generic rather than customer-specific training. In many small and mid-size organizations, there are not any training programs. Perhaps the resources are not available or the need was not readily apparent prior to the decision to begin a quality program.

Subject Matter Experts

There are solutions to both of these situations. The quality trainers must be expanded to include all Subject Matter Experts (SME's) within the organization. These highly skilled, knowledgeable people are the most under-utilized assets in most organizations. Often with little additional training, using the instructional system development method, the SME's will be serving as highly productive trainers in the quality program. SME's from particular work centers can greatly magnify the productive results obtainable from training efforts. An added benefit is that most SME's enjoy training and helping others, they feel honored to be chosen for training duties. Because they help develop their particular programs, their value to the organization increases, which supports them during performance and promotion reviews. This factor makes the training method a true benefit for all who participate.

There are many ways SME's can assist in the quality program. Most importantly, they can conduct all the training for some parts of the quality program. They can assist others in the development of their training programs through technical or organizational input and research. They also can attend or be available for certain parts of training sessions to provide technical expertise. How can these SME's be identified? Some years ago I served as site manager for an engineering, logistics, and technical research operation. We were in the beginning stages of implementing a TQM program. Both necessity and desire made us want to use our own personnel to the maximum extent possible.

The ensuing process became an eye-opener in many ways. It turned out that as an organization, we didn't know very much about our people, and their resumes didn't provide the information we needed. At that point, the decision was made to complete an assets survey. The results were phenomenal. We were sitting on top of a personnel gold mine. (I suspect most other organizations are, too.)

Not only did these employees have talents, knowledge and skills far beyond what we had perceived, it was evident that most of them were anxious to use these attributes to assist fellow employees and the operation.

Skills, Knowledge and Ability in Your Operation

There are four important steps recommended to understand the skills, knowledge and abilities in your operation.[4]

1. Construct a quality assets survey sheet. An example will be provided in the following pages. The survey sheet has proven successful in actual application.

2. Distribute the survey to the employees. We recommend mandatory completion by managers, supervisors, and others in

leadership positions. Each of these individuals was chosen for his/her special skills and should be asked to share those skills with others through training.

3. All other employees should be encouraged to complete a survey. Some workers, with the exception of those mentioned above, may feel they have no special skills. In this case they should not be embarrassed by forcing them to complete a sheet.

3. Review the survey sheets to determine what assets are available. Analyze them carefully. Often those things people tend to forget may be just as important as the ones they choose to include.

4. Interview potential trainers and instructors who possess the required experience or the desire to contribute. Remember, actual classroom training experience is not a must. Effective train-the-trainer instructional programs can be provided which will help most dedicated people become proficient enough to train successfully. Besides, much of the training for quality and process improvement takes place in the workplace, where workers may possess considerable experience. A major way for a trainer to

have an effective program is through good information. One way

to collect this information is through questionnaires.

TQM Questionnaire

We are currently in the process of developing a Total Quality Management (TQM) program. It is our desire to use in-house assets where possible. Nobody knows more about this company than the people working here. Please fill out this questionnaire and return it to your supervisor by _____.

1. Please list your consulting, coaching, training, and mentoring experiences:

2. Please check the subject areas on the following list in which you have knowledge or experience. Additional areas can be added on the reverse side of this form.

___ Training concepts	___ Vision
___ Total quality management	___ Quality goals
___ Supervisory training	___ Planning for quality
___ Management training	___ Implementing quality processes
___ Technical management	___ Quality awareness
___ Project management	___ Employee empowerment
___ Leadership	___ Customer service
___ Team development	___ Sales/marketing techniques
___ Meeting dynamics	___ Management role in quality
___ Change management	___ Work processes
___ Quality environments	___ Process control
___ Conflict resolution	___ Statistical process control
___ Difficult people	___ Performance improvement
___ Participative leadership	___ Job task analysis
___ Delegative leadership	___ The cost of quality
___ Problem solving	___ Quality audits
___ Decision making	___ Drafting a quality manual

___ Using quality tools   ___ Other (list on reverse)
___ Communications

3. Please list any areas where you are willing to serve:

   ___ Quality teams   ___ Program development
   ___ Trainer/instructor   ___ Quality research
   ___ Research   ___ Other (list on reverse)

4. Please list any other ways you are willing to support a Total Quality Management program:

NAME _____ WORK CENTER _____

It is imperative that the person coordinating or directing the Quality Training Program join other managers to negotiate the use of their people. Most will provide the assistance as long as it does not seriously impact on their operational performance. The terms under which other managers support the external use of their people must be clearly understood from the onset. Written confirmation of the agreement should be sent to each manager as a matter of record.

Management Support encourages most SME's to work in the program. The roles and responsibilities of the SME in the quality program must be developed before training is initiated.

Professionalism must be high on the discussion list. Such sessions are a good time to point out the benefits provided by serving as a trainer.

The benefits of being a trainer is that you are able to provide the core values of life and to bring out the ability and character of your students. We hope to see the core of integrity, service before self, and excellence in all we do.

Provide train-the-trainer instructions. Obviously this is an essential evolution. If there is no person available who is capable of obtaining this instruction, outside assistance should be obtained. Organizations such as ASTD and local colleges may provide this training. Many training and consulting firms also provide seminars on this subject. This is one area where penny-pinching can severely limit your ongoing program.

The programs will match trainers to the topics that will be taught and get them started on the development of their part of the training materials. Standardized lesson plans and solid handouts should be a mandatory part of every training session. Without them, the trainer is winging it and the potential to leave out important information; critical steps or safety procedures can prove disastrous results.

Review program assignments with SME's and other trainers at selected intervals to ensure that the development of their training material is on track and that they will be ready on the date they are scheduled to train. There is a human tendency to procrastinate on the development of lesson plans, handouts, and other required training materials. Progress follow-up is necessary; therefore, periodic reviews ensure that the information being issued in the training sessions matches organizational objectives. A teacher's outline is designed to help the trainer prepare a unit. The outline can be written following a balance instruction format. Once the Instructional System Development of any program is implemented all of the steps we discussed will have to be outlined and processed.

The following competencies are addressed by the materials in a train the trainers development program matrix.

X = Supported by module

C = Critical competency

E = Other competency that enhances the specific role

COMPETENCIES:	Training Manager	Trainer	SME
1. Adult Learning Understanding	C	C	E
2. Computer competency	C	C	E
3. Feedback Skill	C	C	C
4. Questioning Skill	E	C	C
5. Presentation Skill	C	E	C
6. Writing Skill	E	C	C
7. Group Process Skill	C	C	E
8. Performance Skill	E	E	C

CHAPTER 9

BENEFITS FROM AN IN-HOUSE TRAINING

PROGRAM

There are a host of payoffs that accrue from a internal training program. These pay offs should be understood because the difference between internal and external programs must be carefully weighed. The following factors considered.[1]

1. Cost – The first and most obvious payoff is program cost. Properly used, internal training resources produce a distinct cost advantage. However, if the training that results from an internal program does not meet organizational performance improvement requirements, the end cost could then become monumental. This program can help you ensure that the cost decision is correctly made.

2. Orientation – The training program will be oriented to the goal. Internal trainers have more knowledge and a significantly higher degree of concern for their organization's vision and strategic

plans. This knowledge and concern provides significant support for quality and performance improvement efforts.

3. Commitment – A successful TQM program demands commitment from the entire workforce. Your personal transition from awareness to involvement, commitment, and ownership are key points in being a part of the internal training team.

4. Team members invest their personal time to prepare training, hold classes, and coach people; they become owners of the training program and the TQM process. As owners, they now have a personal stake in the program's outcome. It becomes theirs. They will invest the necessary effort to ensure they receive a payoff. That is pride of ownership coming through.

5. Self-education – There is no better way to learn a subject than by an assignment to instruct it. The background research, time behind the podium, and interchanges with participants cement ideas. No one learns more in a training situation than the instructor if that instructor truly desires to learn.

6. Leadership Ability – One of the greatest tests of leadership, and one of the biggest builders of leadership skills, is serving as an

instructor, a teacher, or a trainer. Virtually every communication skill is tested and improved. Human relations skill are enhanced continually in ways limited only by the imagination. One soon learns to take charge of the classroom if there is to be a positive outcome.

7. Known Quantities – The people within an organization have known capabilities, personalities and track records. Although some are a known quantities to a certain point; their complete range is unknown until an assets survey has been completed. Workers relate to the training needs because they are part of the team that needs training. Known quantities often makes management more comfortable getting started on quality training because "they are our own people. They think like us because they are us." Team members have a personal stake in the training's outcome. Additionally, trainees relate to these internal trainers because "they are us."

8. Program Standardization – An in-house program has everybody playing off the same sheet of music because it is developed for that institution. This precludes "quality guru chasing" when one

part of the organization follows the dictates of one guru while another follows the dictates of someone else. Those who study the precepts of the various quality experts soon realize they all are in agreement on the need, but are not all in agreement on how to best meet that need. Program Standardization also limits the tendency to "guru-hop" when a program of one guru is started and before it's results can be provided, the decision is made to switch to another program. Both of these tendencies are extremely detrimental to long-term performance improvement.

9. Organization-Centered – An internal program is designed to meet the needs of that organization. Time is not wasted on elements that are not needed within the operation. Program coordinators must ensure that they are programming training to meet all needs. Important areas can be overlooked through ignorance or personal agenda. Therefore both must be guarded against. A comprehensive list of recommended subjects is provided as a guide for a quality curriculum. The Quality Assets checklist is provided for this purpose.

10. Personal Fit – Three universal criteria exist for creating successful training programs. These must be job performance-related, trainee-centered, and (when possible) individually-paced. Trainees learn best when they understand how the training relates to organizational goals and enhanced performance on the job. After all, performance determines such things as job security, pay raises, promotions and self-satisfaction. Because it is job-related, there is an immediate benefit of knowledge and skills, which reinforces training.

All training should be trainee-centered. employee learn best from what they do, not from what the trainer does. It is imperative that the trainee be actively involved in the training to the maximum extent possible. Trainee-paced training is desirable when it is at all possible. This allows each individual to master the material before proceeding on to the next step. This criterion is met through OJT training, computer-based training, interactive video, and self-paced lessons.

11. Personal growth – This final benefit answers the eternal question, "What's in it for me?" Individuals in every organization should

be expanding their resume. This is not to say that everyone should be continually job-hunting; quite the contrary. Resume-building is important as a career development tool in the organization currently being served.

Training experience and the resultant leadership, communications, human relations and other skill improvements has a positive effect on virtually everyone who ever tackles the job. Every organization has room for leaders with training experience. Potential value within the organization is enhanced greatly because successful training provides a visibility individuals probably would not have otherwise seen. The value of this benefit should be stressed from the program's onset because it assists greatly in the quest for volunteers when one is first launching a TQM training program.

CHAPTER 10

NEGATIVE UTILIZATION OF IN-HOUSE

TRAINING SOURCES

There are two sides to every coin, an organization embarking on the quality trip must be aware of potential drawbacks when using internal training sources. These can be overcome by being aware of the seven pit falls below, they say, "forewarned is forewarned."[1]

1. Hesitant training departments or training personnel – Not everyone will heartily endorse Quality Training initiatives. This can be true of almost anyone in the organization, including those involved in training. Many people resist change, especially to an unknown, which TQM usually is. There also may be a hesitancy to share training duties with those outside of the training department. Some folks involved in training may have personal agendas they would rather pursue.

2. Hard work embarking on a new process involves a considerable amount of hard work, which initially can frighten some fainthearted souls.

3. Short on training skills – As mentioned earlier, in-house personnel may have the required technical skills, but lack training skills. This is not an insurmountable problem. Some organizations, however, are not willing to incur the required investments to help their people acquire the necessary training skills. The problem results in ill-prepared trainers who dilute the results of good training material. In some cases, these people do not have the know-how to develop solid lesson plans and materials. This creates an even bigger problem.

4. Lack of knowledge – of latest quality or technical developments. In-house personnel concentrate on those technical developments and quality subjects they perceive as applying directly to their jobs. After all, no one can be expected to know all things about everything. The problem rears its ugly head when the training does not include the latest innovations and knowledge, which puts the organization one step to the rear at the outset. Outside training organizations make it their business to keep abreast of the latest developments. It is their competitive edge.

5. Ineffective ways of completing their efforts – There are untold examples of people doing things the way they have always done them, even though new equipment and technology provides vastly improved methods for increased performance. Example! a large machine shop had recently changed ownership. The new owner was walking through the shop on an initial visit after acquiring it. He noticed several people using an outmoded method of machining an item and proceeded to show them an alternate method which cut production time from 10 hours to a little over an hour and a half. That section's supervisor later discussed this situation with us. He had over 20 years of service with the organization, and in that time they had never received outside training. Procedures were learned on the job from employees with more seniority. With the previous owner no one ever investigated new techniques, however, the new owner mandated it. He subscribed to several publications, brought in a person skilled in the latest technology and methods, and installed a Quality Training program. The employees love it.

6. Lack of time for Research and Program Development – There is only so much time available in each employee's workday. When training, additional responsibilities are added, therefore, something must be subtracted. In many cases there is enough wasted time to allow for these activities. However, management should not automatically assume employees can make time in their schedules for these new assignments and correctly perform all of their old functions as well. Perhaps when the situation is analyzed some employee tasks can be delegated, others can be eliminated altogether Solid training will pay off over time with improved performance, but it won't happen at the start of the program.

7. Lack of commitment to Quality Program – At the onset of initiating quality programs there usually is some hesitancy to commit to the effort. Older workers have watched other programs come and go and they are not that interested in putting considerable additional energy into something that will disappear in six months to a year. It is strongly recommended that personnel who are not committed to the quality program, never be used for

instructors at any level. Those who have suffered through training tragedies put on by people who did not believe in the information they were putting out (and made a point to prove this program wrong at every opportunity) realize how devastating staff can be. A quality program cannot stand this sort of experience.

We will not go into quality implementation with a hopeless attitude. This attitude tends to be a initial learning opportunities that disappears rather quickly given time, management effort, and leadership from the top. Once management is on board, most of the employees are willing to give the program a chance.

CHAPTER 11

CORPORATE TRAINING AS A FORM OF

ANOTHER IN-HOUSE TRAINING PROGRAM

Corporate Universities

While the word "university" conjures up thoughts of ivy-covered building and tenured faculty, the corporate version is very different. As a group, 1,000 corporate universities are emerging as innovators in the design and delivery of high-quality on-demand education. They are using distance learning technologies to bring learning to the workplace; forming collaborations with local, international and virtual universities; and developing tools so employees can share their best practices.

What does the future of learning look like at these corporate universities? Each year Corporate University Xchange, Inc. conducts a survey of 100 corporate university deans, known as the Annual Survey of Corporate University Future Directions.[1] We asked this group of university deans to share their best practices with us. Following is a discussion of five of the top-line findings:[2]

135

A growing number of organizations have created the job of chief learning officer, the chief strategist of the corporate university responsible for linking education to critical business strategies. The Annual Survey of Corporate University Future Directions found that almost 20 percent of these Chief Learning Officers report directly to the CEO, and this trend is expected to grow as more companies view corporate education as a partner in achieving critical business goals.

At companies with corporate universities, top management is becoming increasingly committed to and involved in the learning process. CEOs at companies included in the survey spend an average of one day each month facilitating learning programs. General Motors University is going one step beyond involving the CEO, by partnering with the Center for Creative Leadership in training 2,000 mid-level executives in General Motors's vision, values and leadership competencies. This type of role modeling demonstrates the commitment that leaders have to the learning process.[3]

Learning solutions combine high-tech with high-touch and result in fun, entertainment and engaging programs. The Survey of Corporate University Future Directions found that while less than 20 percent of learning is currently delivered using technology, 100 corporate university deans predict that by the year 2000 this will grow to more than 50 percent. In addition, the greatest area of growth is seen to be education delivered over corporate intranets. The sample indicates that intranets will account for over one-third of all training delivered via technology.

Corporations are increasingly developing joint degree programs with institutions of higher education. The survey found that 40 percent of corporate universities plan to grant degrees in partnership with an accredited institution of higher education. These degrees are primarily at the graduate level in business administration, engineering, finance and computer science.

The main driver of this interest in offering accredited learning programs is the desire to grant portable credentials as part of the corporate training program. Rather than automatically fund tuition reimbursement programs, organizations with corporate universities are proactive in specifying the types of skills and knowledge needed for success in an industry.

Finally, the Survey of Corporate University Future Directions indicates a strong interest in having the corporate university become a profit center by leveraging its organization's "brand name" and reputation for business excellence.[4] By applying consumer product branding techniques to the corporate education arena, corporate universities are taking the best of their own corporate training programs and marketing them to outsiders.

Another survey from *Training & Development*, July 1999, provides the point of view from the Corporate University aspect of learning.

Three strong trends – an increase in continuous learning among working adult students, the growth in Internet-based learning, and dissatisfaction by business leaders with the status quo of higher education – have combined to fuel a growing interest in corporate universities. The number of corporate universities has increased dramatically over the last 10 years from 400 in 1998 to more than 1,600 in 1999.

If the current pace of growth continues, by 2010 the number of corporate universities will exceed the number of traditional universities, according to the survey results released by Corporate University Xchange INC.. Overwhelmingly, the top driver for launching a corporate university is to improve employee performance and productivity. Forty percent of Fortune 500 companies have instituted corporate universities.

Other findings of the survey indicates that:

Corporate Universities budgets and external sales are on the rise. The average operating budget for a corporate university has increased from $13 million to $17 million. "External sales" is defined as receiving funding from outside the organization; 25 percent of the corporate universities surveyed receive such funds. By 2003, that figure is expected to increase to 43 percent.

CEOs are becoming role models and advocates for employee learning. Corporate Universities are increasingly being recognized as a means of enhancing competitive advantage and attracting and retaining employees. Tight labor forces are driving companies to invest in training and retaining current staff. Consequently, corporate universities are attracting the attention of CEOs and Senior Managers in a number of ways. For example, the survey found that 83 percent of the CEOs at responding companies mention corporate universities in their speeches, and 59 percent feature it in the company's annual report. Further, 34 percent of CEOs are teaching a course in the corporate university. Since technology is becoming a crucial vehicle for learning delivery, a key function of the corporate university is to deliver education through myriad technologies in order to provide staff with access to on-demand education and development. Statistics are:

- 93 percent of respondents use learning technologies to deliver training and education.
- 82 percent use some form of Web-based technology.
- 41 percent expect to use <u>extranets</u> for delivery by 2003.
- 20 percent of learning is currently delivered through technology; that figure is expected to reach 44 percent by 2003.

The last finding:

- Corporations are increasing partnerships with universities and technology firms.

Corporate universities are expanding their partnerships with distance learning vendors; while 61 percent currently have such partnerships, the number is expected to increase to 80 percent by 2003. Among established corporate universities (operating for 10 years or more), 92 percent have developed strategic partnerships among distance learning vendors.

More than 50 percent of the surveyed companies with corporate universities said they're planning to grant degrees in partnership with an accredited institution. The most sought-after degrees are in such areas as business, management, engineering, computer science, finance and accounting.

Business is applying their corporate learning expertise in creating a new learning organization within their own companies. To compete with global corporations meeting the challenge of tomorrows improving human performance in the workplace.

BLUEWATER UNIVERSITY

We will cover a few different businesses and organizations that use the corporate university format for training. The first one we will look at is the Bluewater University, where I was Director Of Business and Customer Service.

Bluewater University, established in 1995, is the 96th Services Squadron formal customer service education and staff development program for employees located at Eglin Air Force Base, Florida.[5] While it is modeled after some academic institutions and parallels other military base programs, it has been developed using input from all employees as a basis for our initial academic offerings.

Through survey activity visits and interactions with employees, supervisors and management, a core of required courses was developed. The four-phase program developed as an integrated process of solutions to problems, employee development and customer satisfaction is hereafter referred to as degrees. Each degree is further refined and leads to employee achievement and recognition by award of a squadron diploma. Requirements for satisfactory completion of course work leading to a degree are listed in the awarding of degree section of Bluewater's handbook.

The intent of Bluewater University is to make education and training a continuous process and not a burden to employees or supervisors. The purpose of Bluewater University is to assist personnel to develop into productive, customer-oriented, quality-focused, profit-conscious employees.[6]

To this end the following goals were established:

1. Establish a quality learning environment.

2. Enhance ongoing programs and employee job satisfaction.

3. Teach all employees how to perform superior quality service.

4. Provide opportunities to learn or refresh skills and knowledge.

5. Foster better relationships between managers, supervisors and employees.

6. Maintain high standards of personal and instructional professionalism, academic preparation and government experience.

7. Develop an academic advisement service to each student, supervisor and manager on a continuing basis to facilitate progression toward customer service educational goals.

8. Develop options, within the limit of resources, available to enhance teaching and learning activities.

9. Maintain alternatives to traditional classroom delivery systems by enhancing programs, utilizing or sponsoring workshops, and courses in liaison with the civilian and military community.

10. Provide accurate educational and training records for degree certification and as a source documentation for future use of the students.

In addition to overall objectives and goals we endeavor:

To encourage and reward excellence in instructors.

To provide essential support services for activities and research that is creative.

To seek out and develop continuing educational programs that enable students to read, write, compute, speak and think critically in dealing with our customers.

To prepare students to demonstrate competence and excellence at the appropriate degree levels in customer service education.

To provide leadership and planning for future development.

Their statement is "we are dedicated to provide a cohesive program of customer service, education, with an emphasis on personal attention to our students by both faculty and staff."

Motorola University Corporation

Motorola University is the in-house training facility for all levels of education within Motorola with operations globally at facilities in Schaumberg, Illinois; Phoenix, Arizona; Austin, Texas; Singapore; Yokohama, Japan; and Tianjin and Beijing, China.[7]

The vision of Motorola University is: "Dedicated to the continuous education of every Motorola employee."

Traditionally Motorola University has been charged with changing the mind of Motorola. The university is to make Motorola think, be challenged, and to preserve the culture through relaying it to new generations of employees. The process of developing curriculum systems is essentially to map initiatives.

In order to be successful in mapping, Motorola University needs to be creative in its methods of communication; e.g., in the '90s, resources were allocated for translation initiatives. While Motorola University trains across all levels, the discussions focused on more senior level and executive training.

The mission of Motorola University is to be a major catalyst for change and continuous improvement in support of the corporation's business objectives. They will provide clients the best value, leading-edge training, and education solutions and systems in order to be their preferred partner in developing a Best in Class workforce.[8] Basically business units do not have to send staff to Motorola University.

Motorola University is structured into colleges with separate missions and handling separate levels of development of staff.

College of Leadership and Trans cultural Studies: The mission is to make lasting and distinctive contributions to Motorola's worldwide business through leadership development and management education. This college handles specific programs at First Level, Middle

Manager, Director and Executive Education.[9] Specifically at Executive Education level, the overall key themes for 1997 in this college were Totality of Motorola Learning, Value Creation, Culture, Organizational Renewal and Business Ethics.

Also included within this college are the MBA program and the "Business Laboratory" concept for case study work on Motorola cases. Teamwork is strongly implemented in all of these courses for benchmarking, sharing of functional knowledge, adopting a "Think Tank" and Developing knowledge management.

Lesson From Business Education At Motorola:

Motorola is one of the most ambitious corporations in the job-training movement today. Motorola believes that the company's sizable training commitment has contributed to strong financial results. Motorola delivers a minimum of 40 hours of training to each of its 139,000 employees. Productivity measured per employee has climbed significantly with the commitment to training. Motorola considers its emphasis on continuous education a crucial advantage in today's marketplace.

Motorola's training program is considered a model in corporate circles because of its strong link to the company's business strategy – this Motorola considers critical. The company trains to solve performance problems.[10]

Many traditional universities could learn from Motorola University with the way company managers help shape the training curriculum based on their specific needs. Courses are not designed in a vacuum and imposed from the top down. Rather, design intimately involves managers and employees from a bottom-up approach.

Employee training is now so deeply ingrained at Motorola that every employee, from top executive to factory worker, is responsible for identifying courses he or she wants to study each year.

Indicative of the approach of Motorola to continuing education is the plan to double its education efforts over the next five years. By the end of the decade, every worker will study 80 to 100 hours per year. The overall critical lessons to learn from Motorola are not to over-train the employees, but to critically align educational efforts with business needs.

Education and Training as a Competitive Advantage

Many corporations should consider the philosophy of Motorola

and the training of its Motorolas for competitive advantage. In view

of the importance of this area, the Motorola philosophy of education

and training as competitive advantage is outlined below.[11]

EDUCATION AND TRAINING AS A COMPETITIVE

ADVANTAGE

Best in Class Workforce	Entry into New/ Potential Markets	Training/Education Key Component of the Value Chain
Education system alliances K to 16 initiatives Learning apprenticeships Continual upgrade of knowledge and skills Competency-focused Business-driven Future/strategically directed Five-day training policy	Government, public agency, market development initiatives University partnerships Research Joint ventures Shared resources Value-added competencies Instructional design expertise Courses and materials Facilities and professional staff Customer and supplier training	Quality of work force products Benchmarking opportunities Host international visitors Customers Governments Universities Understand/interpret/ support cultural diversity Incentive to purchase using Motorola University services Accepted as value-added component for Motorola businesses

Motorola considers the keys to successful training and education to be:

- Philosophy of organizational learning

- Top-down commitment and involvement

- Linkage of programs to corporate initiatives

- Policies that set expectations and are tracked

- Solid prerequisite skills of the workforce

- Curricula that forms an integrated system to deliver consistent messages

The overall benchmark training model for Motorola is:

Person + Training + Time +Environment = Effective TRAINING

The techniques of theses models bring us to the following results.

Conclusions:

- The need for continuous education for all levels of employees of an organization and recognition of the potential return on investment for education.

- The new methods of delivery of education, e.g., distant and satellite learning, and the efficiency of these new learning processes need to be carefully evaluated as they can be delivered efficiently. The relevance and appropriateness of such courses to corporate conditions and workplace situations will need to be evaluated.

- What does corporate industry consider as their need for continuous education in the future?

Regents College Corporate University

Regents University removes barriers – such as residency requirements, nontransferable credits, and inconvenient class schedules – that prevent working adults from furthering their education.[12]

"We are America's first virtual university," says Dr. Leader, "but our view of the virtual university is that it's more than on-line courses. It recognizes learning wherever and whenever it occurs. We connect students with learning opportunities and award credit for the learning that takes place." Academic requirements at Regents are determined by 350 faculty members from around the country, almost all of whom are senior, tenured faculty at their home campuses.

"We are very traditional in the standards and criteria we have for awarding credit. It's just that we make learning – and credit for learning – more accessible to more people," says Dr. Leader.

In the last several years it has become a well-established fact that accessible education and lifelong learning are necessary for businesses to maintain a competitive advantage. By extension of education, lifelong learning on a national scale must take hold to ensure that America remains a nation of opportunity and a powerful force in the global economy. None of this is news to Regents College. They've been doing their part for a quarter of a century by developing new pathways to learning for adults. Regents will continue to play a significant role in workforce development, lifelong learning and the development of innovative ways to bring college-level learning to busy, working adults.

CHAPTER 12

A QUICK LOOK AT A FEW TRAINING

PROGRAMS WITH MAJOR COMPANIES

Hotels & Resorts

The first corporation we will look at is called hospitality A. Hospitality A is committed to doing business in a way that empowers all employees to work toward continuous product innovation and improvement, thereby ensuring maximum quality and service to all guests, employees, and owners.[1]Hospitality A is a corporation in the service industry with numerous properties nationwide. To this corporation total Quality is not a training program, but a carefully designed training plan necessary to ensure that people have the right skills and knowledge to carry out it's total quality objectives and goals. Some of these skills are people-oriented; for example, how to work in teams. Some of these skills prepare people to analyze processes and interpret data. A training plan will ensure that the right people get the right training at the right time.

Using a Total Quality Training matrix as a guide, management determines what training different groups of employees at each property will need to support achieving their goals.[2] Training will be different for each property. Although, training can be provided by Hospitality A, will be necessary to take advantage of regional, local and property-based opportunities to fulfill their training needs.

Hospitality A approached the training itself in three phases. First, facilitator training for the leaders of the quality improvement teams, provided locally and as appropriate.

Second, long-term training for the total quality leader provided by a national source. Third, every associate received a basic orientation to Total Quality Hospitality by the end of 1993. They focused on providing "just in time" training, not "just in case" training. Initially, they looked for ways to use people with the most total quality information and experience to provide training, e.g., General Manager, and Total Quality Leader.[3] Their belief was to combine training with other local organizations or regionally connected Hospitality A properties.

Hospitality A believes training shouldn't be a random event. It should be A planned it out and implemented process within your organization. The "givens" for training is within the five-step Continuous Improvement Process and the. Training that is implemented must be compatible with these givens.

1. Continuous improvement: Every Hospitality A employee is involved in a daily search for improvements in all services, products, and organizational processes.

2. Employee involvement and teamwork: Every employee participated in establishing and achieving total quality improvement goals.

3. Customer-centered: The primary job of every employee is to satisfy or exceed customer expectations.

4. Data-based decision making: Employees use data to understand, measure and improve the quality of products, processes and services.

5. Systems and support: All organizational systems and supports are designed to improve the ability to drive continuous process improvements and increase customer satisfaction.

6. Top management ownership: Every senior manager is personally empowered, visibly involved, and held accountable for developing, leading and sustaining an environment that supports Total Quality Management.

7. Supplier involvement: Demands from suppliers the same commitment and adherence to quality standards that is demanded from itself.

Figure 12-1. SAMPLE TRAINING MATRIX*

Skill/Knowledge Area	GMs	Quality Council	TQ Leads	Managers	All Employees	Facilitators	Trainers	Team Leaders	Team Members
TQ Tools: Interview								X	X
Interpersonal communications	X	X	X	X		X	X	X	X
Orientation to TQ at Westin	X	X	X	X	X	X	X	X	X
Data: Measuring, tracking, and analysis: In-depth	X	X	X	X		X	X		
5-Step Continuous Improvement Process	X	X	X	X		X	X	X	X
Identifying customers, their needs, and expectations	X	X	X	X		X	X		
Managing meetings	X	X	X	X		X	X	X	

This is a sample. It is not intended as a complete list of skills and knowledge for TQ implementation.

Manufacturing "A" Training

Manufacturing "A" believes in thorough competency-based training, and one of their slogans is "we will become what our competitors believe we can't." Truly competitive Manufacturing "A" has five phases of training. They are:

1. Everybody has a training plan.[4]

2. Training has a demonstrable impact on job performance.

3. Training is looked on as an investment, not a cost.

4. Training is driven by the needs of the organization.

5. A high percentage of people are involved in providing training.

Manufacturing "A" training plan is laid out in a step-by-step process for the best results. Their culture consists of labor management partnership, empowered teams (ownership), system views, information sharing, risk and reward sharing, and Training Lifelong Learning.[5]

Their program uses a curriculum evolution that consists of the following items.[6]

- Orientation and awareness

- Computer literacy – keyboard skill

- Time management

- Instructional design

- Decision making

- Managing conflict

Curriculum Evolution

- Seven basic habits of highly effective people

- Technical committees

- Quality overview

- Leader specific

- Strategy specific (interviewer)

- Team building/Excel

- Equipment specific

- Process specific

- Operator certification

Manufacturing "A" process is built around training. They develop strategic direction and analyze the needs of the company. They acquire or design/develop training, and very important processes that are verified and evaluated. Manufacturing "A" uses training development teams and uses task analysis to enhance their learning objectives. Another important step is their train-the-Trainer Process, which increases staff trainers. The corporation has built a program to administer training to include training facilities, delivering training by way of (facilitators, coaches), and measuring and evaluating training to implement hiring and training measurements. This program is vast and has many areas to identify improvement that fit right into Manufacturing "A" training initiatives.

Their training initiatives are as follows:

- Grow Manufacturing "A" University

- Assist with growth of GM University

- Integrate QS 9000 (Auto. ISO 9000)

- Improve measurement/evaluation process

- Grow distance learning

- Grow computer-based/in-house training

- Benchmark new approaches in learning

This is the point where we will call it a point of comparison. I have provided my opinion of a true look at what is available for the in-house trainer. I have touched on just a few In- house training programs that include distance learning, satellite training, and computer-based training. There are many more items that can be considered in accreditation and certification. For corporate training beyond the scope of this book.

CONCLUSION

Closing Statement of the Paper

This book is an examination of Quality Management training programs. It gives us quite a look into dealing with these programs. I have explained this holistic step-by-step process of creating and implementing a training program with different elements necessary to perform this action, that include research and input I received from companies in the quality training business. Some of the letters I received provided excellent information which contributed to completion of this book. I would also like to discuss some of the data I didn't use in the body of this project.

A reply from Gary A. Krull & Associates, Inc. who informed me that his company is diversified in many areas of quality. Training is one of their areas of expertise. The majority of their business is contracted through marketing, networking and referrals. They contract as International Standardization Organization (ISO)/Quality Standard (QS 9000) Global Certified Auditors through National and International Accredited Registration, ISO/QS Certified Plexus

Trainers, Quality Management Consultants, and quality system implementation. They enclosed a training plan for a proposal for training 90 personnel in Statistical Process Control.

The Quality Breakthrough of Brainerd, MN send me a letter saying they operate using a virtual organization and, therefore, do all their training externally. There were many other letters, some saying I am asking too much, or not asking the right questions, and further suggested I refine the phraseology; e.g., do you mean "Quality in-house training" or "Quality in the house training," and many other statements. I will stay on the positive and cover one more reply that I found very helpful: DM Stowell & Company Management, Marketing, Quality Consulting. This is a two-person consulting firm, and as such does not have an in-house training program. However, the firm does provide quality training to their clients, and they do have an understanding of their clients' in-house and external training programs.

They asked if I was trying to identify the effect of quality training on company operations. My response was no. Training is rarely the most important factor in the success of a quality improvement effort.

The most important factor is the commitment, support and active participation of top management. Their last statement was that they would be interested in the results of my research. They are involved with the Quality Management Division of the American Society for Quality, and they are looking for material for their newsletter and annual conference.

This is saying that training often does not receive the respect, support and involvement from management many believe it should, and there can be good reason for this lack of management support. In many instances, training is focused on the training itself and not on helping the organization change in a measurable way. The goal on the minds of the worlds business executives is how to get better business results, including improving the bottom line. This should be the focus of professionals who provide training for all organizations and agencies.

Internal and external customers have complained for years that management doesn't support training. Training events get cancelled or postponed to make room for priorities. Training budgets are the first to get sliced when the economic is weak. Management participation should be involved in training sessions no matter where it's led by a training professional or a contractor. Often training is viewed by the whole organization, not just management, as a cost, not an investment that will produce a positive return to the bottom line. Many more believe that business is not getting its money worth out of training. For this to change, the mind – set of management and training professionals must take the lead in bringing this change about. Using continuous improvement processing for change is what we should evaluate. By doing this, it is not unusual for a project, through improvements identified and made early in the project's life, to return bottom – line saving that more than pay for the cost of training before the training is complete.

Many organizations and agencies create training budgets that look at training the same way they would look at utility consumption. If utility costs are high, the company looks to reduce costs. In the same way, companies also try to reduce training budgets over time. Certainly some training is completely mandated by various authorities, therefore, this expense is considered a fixed cost. Management should review a lot of it's training, to determine its value as an investment. Management should not ask how it can cut training by 10%, but rather what the internal rate of return (IRR) on the training for the past year is, and how it can increase the IRR next year. Companies should focus on improvement not training itself. It is of little value to train people just to say we did so. Management must train to build the skills that improve processes, and make the organization better. All training should have a clear, measurable business objective connected to the bottom line.

Another result I arrived at from this information is that we are at the beginning of a great movement in quality training. The question is how can organizations will use these approaches to create great in-house training programs. Quality Management leads companies toward the holistic process of training for the purpose of developing it's people. The sources of training, through evaluation, laid a background toward providing training.

Quality improvement and the tools for making decisions diagramed the necessary data input used to provide these techniques. A key part is to instill the knowledge so quality assessment training will become an element of an organization leading the way to designing a quality culture for the purpose of achieving company goals.

The implementation of a quality training plan and the benefits received from an in-house training program are step-by-step methods to success. Corporate universities as a form of in-house training programs is an area that has been around for a while. Studies are showing it will continue to become a future source that business will tap into for growth. I contacted many corporations and received information on their training programs. My experience and data I have received tell me that an in-house training program can be used by all businesses. There are training materials that may be purchased and applied to small or large companies, enabling them to implement and run a training program with minimal cost. The larger the company, the more the cost per employee; however. This is a concept is that should be looked at, as the return on investment will be much larger than the cost.

All organizations should have an training program. Because knowledge is power, and power is within the people.

QM TRAINING GLOSSARY OF TERMS

ASSIGNABLE CAUSE – a factor that contributes to variation and is feasible to detect and identify.

AVERAGE – the sum of values divided by the number (sample set) of values.

BENCHMARKING – rating a company's practices, processes and products against the world's best, including those in other industries.

BRAINSTORMING – a group technique for generating new and useful ideas.

CAUSE-AND-EFFECT DIAGRAM – a visual display of the suggested causal relationships among theories. Also called "fishbone" diagram or Ishikawa diagram. Used when you need to identify, explore and display the possible causes of a specific problem or condition.

CHECKLIST – a list of actions or items to be reviewed during a process; the actions or items are "checked off" as they are completed or identified.

CHECKSHEET – a form for collecting data. The completed form displays the data in a simple graphic summary. Used when you need to gather data based on sample observation in order to begin to detect patterns.

CLASS – a group of values that describe some characteristic of the data. Also called an interval. One reason grouping is done is to conduct histograms and to interpret data.

CONTINUOUS IMPROVEMENT PROCESS – a structured process used to continually improve the quality of processes, products, service and organizational relationships. The Japanese call it Kaizen.

CONTROL CHARTS – statistical plots that help detect "process drift" or deviation before it causes defects. A control chart is a run chart with statistically determined upper (upper control limit) and possibly lower (lower control limit) lines drawn on either side of the process average. Used when you need to discover how much variability in a process is due to random variation and how much is due to unique events/individual actions in order to determine whether a process is in statistical control.

CUSTOMERS – the people who receive and use the results of your work, whether that is a service or a physical product. Everyone has customers, and they may be external or internal.

DATA POINT – an individual measurement.

FLOW CHART – a graphic representation of the steps in a process. Also called a flow diagram or flow map.

HISTOGRAM – a graphic summary of the variation in a set of data. Used when you need to discover and display the distribution of data by bar graphing the number of units in each category.

JUST IN TIME – when suppliers deliver materials and parts at the moment they are needed, thus eliminating costly inventories.

LINE GRAPH – a series of line segments connecting points of paired numeric data, representing the functional relationship between the two variables.

MEAN – the average of values in a group of measurements.

MEASUREMENT – the act or process of measuring to obtain a value from characteristics of interest. The value obtained is called a measurement.

MEDIAN – the middle value in a group of measurements when it is arranged from lowest to highest.

MISSION STATEMENT – a problem statement given to a process improvement team along with management's direction on what objectives the team should fulfill with respect to improving the process.

MODE – the most frequent value in a group of measurements.

NEEDS ASSESSMENT – an audit providing the background information for the entire training program.

PARETO ANALYSIS – a ranked comparison of factors related to a quality problem. It separates the "vital few" from the "useful many."

PARETO CHART – a bar graph that ranks causes of process variation by the degree of impact on quality. Used when you need to display the relative importance of all problems or conditions in order to choose the starting point for problem solving, monitor success, or identify the basic cause of a problem.

PROCESS – the combination of people, raw materials, methods, machines and equipment, and environments that produces a given service or product. Every work activity is part of a process.

PROCESS IMPROVEMENT TEAM – a group of people assigned the responsibility of diagnosing and remedying a quality problem associated with a process.

RUN CHART – a visual representation of data used to monitor a process to see whether or not the long-range average is changing. Used when you need to do the simplest possible display of trends within observation points over a specified time period.

QUALITY CIRCLES – groups of people, usually from the same work area, who meet regularly on a voluntary basis to identify, analyze, and solve quality and other problems in their area.

QUALITY CULTURE – an organization with a built-in value system that results in an environment that is conducive to the establishment and continual improvement of quality.

QUALITY FUNCTION DEPLOYMENT (QFD) – a system that pays special attention to customer wants. Activities that don't contribute are considered wasteful.

QUALITY IMPROVEMENT – a structured process for the reduction and elimination of chronic waste associated with poor quality.

RANGE – the difference between the highest and lowest values in a set of values.

SCATTER DIAGRAM – graphic representation of the observed relationship between two variables. Used when you need to display what happens to one variable when another variable changes in order to test a theory that the two variables are related.

STANDARD DEVIATION – a measure of the spread of the process output or the spread of a sampling statistic from the process.

SYMPTOM – a specific observed evidence of a quality problem.

THEORY – an unproved statement about what the root cause of a quality problem might be.

TOTAL QUALITY MANAGEMENT (TQM) – the application of quality principles to all company endeavors, including satisfying internal "customers." Also known as total quality control (TQC).

TRAINING – an organized, systematic series of activities designed to enhance an individual's work-related knowledge, skills, understanding and/or motivation.

TRENDS – patterns in a Run Chart or Control Chart that indicate a rise or fall in a series of points.

VARIATION – the difference among individual outputs of a process. The sources of variation are grouped into two major classes: Common Causes and Special Causes.

TOTAL QUALITY MANAGEMENT
SELECTED BIBLIOGRAPHY

Abella, K.T. *Building Successful Training Programs.* Reading, Mass: Addison Wesley,
1986.

Biech, E. *TQM For Training.* New York: McGraw-Hill, 1994.

Betts, L.M. Saturn Training Report, 1998.

Bowles, J., and J. Hammond. Beyond Quality: How 50 Winning Companies Use Continuous Improvement, Englewood Cliff is NJ: Prentice – Hall. 1991.

Brinkerhoff, R.O. *Achieving Results from Training.* San Francisco: Jossey-Bass, 1987.

Broadwell, M.M. *The Supervisor and On-the-Job Training.* Reading, Mass: Addison-Wesley, 1986.

Camp, R.C. Benchmarking: The Search for Industry Best Practices that Lead to Superior Performance, 1989.

Deming, W.E. *Out of the Crisis*, Mass: Massachusetts Institute of Technology, 1989.

Goetsch, D.L. and Stanley B. Davis. Introduction to Total Quality, 1994.

Goldratt, E.M. and Jeff Cox. The Goal: A Process of Ongoing Improvement, 1986.

Guaspari, J. I Know It When I See It: A Modern Fable About Quality, 1985.

Imai, M. Kaisen: The Key to Japan's Competitive Success, 1986.

Ishikawa, K. Guide to Quality Control, Englewood Cliff, Prentice – Hall, 1976.

Jablonski, J.R. Implementing Total Quality Management, 1991.

Kume, H. Statistical Methods for Quality Improvement, 1985.

Mitchell, G. *The Trainer's Handbook.* New York: American Management Association, 1987.

Rummier G.A., Alan P. Brache. Improving Performance: How to Manage the White Space on the Organization Chart, 1990.

Scholtes, P.R. *The Team Handbook.* Madison, Wisc: Joiner Associates Inc., 1992.

Weaver, C.N. TQM, Step-by-Step Guide to Implementation, Quality Press Milwaukee Wisconsin. 1991.

Zeithaml, V.A., A. Parasuraman, and L.L. Berry. Delivering Quality Service: Balancing Customer Perceptions and Expectations, 1990.

Larry Anderson

NOTES

CHAPTER 1

1. Percy L. Johnson, *Total Quality Management* (Southfield, Michigan: Percy Johnson Inc., 1991), 1-1.

2. Stephen Uselac, *Zen Leadership: The Human Side of Total Quality Management* (Loudonville, Ohio: Mohicon Publishing Company, 1991), 20.

3. Air Force Development Test Center, *Total Quality Management (TQM) Training Package* (1991), 8.

4. Jerry Romano, "It's Time for a Quality Management Revolution" Workshop presented to the Emerald Coast Personnel Managers Association (1992).

5. Ibid.

6. Ibid.

7. Air Force Air University, *Process Improvement Guide* (1993), 91.

8. Peter R. Scholtes, *The Team Handbook* (Madison, Wisconsin: Joiner Associates Inc., 1992), 1-11.

9. Johnson, 5.

10. National Center for Manufacturing Sciences, *Focus* (August 1992), 8.

11. Ibid.

12. Edward W. Deming. *Out of the Crisis* (Cambridge Massachusetts, Massachusetts Institute of Technology, 1989), 30.

CHAPTER 2

1. Dick Schaaf, "The Changing Role of Training: From Rage to Riches" (Corporate Development in the '90s: Supplement to Training, 1991), 5.

2. Ibid.

3. John Hoerr, "Business Shares the Blame for Workers' Low Skill," *Business Week*, 25 June 1990, 71.

4. National Center for Manufacturing Sciences, *Focus* (August 1992), 8.

5. Tom Peters, *Thriving on Chaos: Handbook for a Management Revolution* (New York: Harper & Row Publishers, 1987), 386.

6. Nell P. Eurich, *Corporate Classroom: The Learning Business* (Lawrenceville, New Jersey: Princeton University Press, 1995).

7. Gilda Dangot-Simpkin, "How to Get What You Pay For," *Training*, July 1990, 53-54.

8. Joseph M. Juran, *Juran on Leadership for Quality: An Executive Handbook* (New York: The Free Press, 1989), 323-27.

CHAPTER 3

1. Joseph M. Juran, *Juran on Leadership for Quality: An Executive Handbook* (New York: The Free Press, 1989), 323-37.

2. Ibid., 336.

3. Ibid., 337.

4. Elaine Biech, *TQM for Training* (New York: McGraw Hill, 1994), 51.

5. Instruction for Design of Instructional System Design Training, Handbook 1 November 1993 Department of Defense.

CHAPTER 4

1. Air Force Quality Institute. Process Improvement Guide, Quality tools For Teams And Individuals, Air University Maxwell A.F.B., Alabama (1990), 5-10.

2. Air Force Quality Center

3. Air Force Quality Institute, Tools For Generating Ideas, 5-12.

4. Ibid., Tools For Making Decisions, 15.

5. Ibid., Group Technique, 17.

6. Ibid., Tools For Analyzing Problems, 25.

7. Ibid., Flow Diagrams, 29.

8. Ibid., Stratification Analysis, 34.

CHAPTER 5

Air Force Quality Center Process Improvement Guide, Quality Tools For Today's Air Force, Maxwell AFB, AL. 1993

CHAPTER 6

1. Lloyd Dobyns and Crawford Mason, *Quality or Else: The Revolution in World Business* (New York: Houghton Mifflin Company, 1991), 275.

2. Terrence E. Deal and Allen A. Kennedy, *Corporate Cultures, Perseus Books Group New york, New york, 1998*

3. Joseph M. Juran, *Juran on Leadership* (New York: The Free Press, 1989), 184.

4. Dobyns, 275.

5. Juran, 317-319.

6. Ibid., 317.

7. David Hollis, "Total Quality, Culture Change and Facilitation" (Internet article). http://www.3.mistrat.co.uk/dhollis/forward.htm

8. Stanley B. Davis, *Implementing TQM* Prentice – Hall Columbus, Ohio. (1997). P 609

CHAPTER 7

1. Costa and McRae, *Five Factor Model of Personality The Guilford Press New York, London,* (1998), 1-10.

2. D.P. McAdams, "The Five-Factor Model in Personality: A Critical Appraisal," *Journal of Personality*, 1992.

CHAPTER 8

1. Richard S. Johnson, *Quality Training Practices* ASQC Quality Press Milwaukee Wisconsin, (1993), 63-71

2. M.M. Broadwell, *The Supervision of On-the-Job Training* (Reading, MA: Addison-Wesley), 1986.

3. K.T. Abella. *Building Successful Training Programs* (Reading, MA: Addison-Wesley), 1986.

4. P.A. McLagan, *Helping Others Learn* (Reading, MA: Addison-Wesley), 1978.

CHAPTER 9

1. R.L. Craig, ed., *American Society for Training and Development: Training Development Handbook* (New York, NY: McGraw-Hill), 1976.

CHAPTER 10

1. R.O. Brinkerhoff, *Achieving Results from Training* (San Francisco, CA: Jossey-Boss), 1987, 72.

CHAPTER 11

1. Corporate University article. Available at: http://www.corp.com/98CEBS/cux2.html.

2. Ibid., 1-2.

3. Ibid., 1-3.

4. Ibid., 1-2.

5. Mike Devins, *Bluewater University Handbook* (Fort Walton Beach FL: Eglin AFB), 1995, 1-11.

6. Ibid.

7. Carl Lund, *Garth Rynmer, Motorola Corporation Marketing.* Available at: ccinz/800/staff/business/company reports/ Motorola.html, 1990, 1. http:// Marketing.Otago.ac.nz: 800 / marketing / staff/buisson/company Reports/ Motorola .html

8. Ibid., 2.

9. Ibid.

10. Ibid., 4.

11. Ibid., 6.

12. Chari Leader, PhD, *Internet Fortune*. Available at: section.com/corporate universities/cu7.html. http:// www. Fortune – Sections.com/corporateuniversities/ cut.htm/

CHAPTER 12

1. Ibid., 8, Appendix B.

2. Ibid., 8.

3. Lesa McClain Betts, *Training at Saturn* (Spring Hill, Tennessee), 1997, 1.

4. Ibid., 3.

5. Ibid., 7.

6.

ABOUT THE AUTHOR

Dr. Larry J. Anderson began his organizational development, diversity, and management career in the early eighties. Dr. Anderson received a Ph.D. in business management with an emphasis in quality management from Barrington University. His master's degree in management science is from Troy State University. He completed a bachelor's degree in vocational education from Southwest Texas State University. Dr. Anderson has also received certification as a quality management facilitator from the University of West Florida for implementation of quality programs to public and private organizations. He provides organizational consultation, and has conducted training programs that have successfully been implemented in both business and government entities. Dr. Anderson participated as a facilitator for the Defense Equal Opportunity Management Institute (DEOMI) certifying equal opportunity advisors.

He was proud that he had a successful career in the United Air Force. Dr. Anderson serves as a member of the American Society for

Quality (ASQ), American Society for Training and Development (ASTD), magnifying his briefing, seminars, and training sessions.

Printed in the United Kingdom
by Lightning Source UK Ltd.
103027UKS00002B/69